9-14-97

'96-64/270

+

UNIVERSITY OF NORTH CAROLINA
STUDIES IN THE ROMANCE LANGUAGES AND LITERATURES
Number 57

SPANISH LIFE IN THE LATE MIDDLE AGES

SPANISH LIFE IN THE LATE MIDDLE AGES

SELECTED AND TRANSLATED

BY

KENNETH R. SCHOLBERG

CHAPEL HILL

THE UNIVERSITY OF NORTH CAROLINA PRESS

PRINTED IN SPAIN

DEPÓSITO LEGAL: V. 2.504 - 1965

ARTES GRÁFICAS SOLER, S. A. — VALENCIA. — 1965

FOREWORD

The life and reign of King Juan II of Castile extended approximately over the first half of the fifteenth century (1405-1454) and is in many ways one of the most fascinating periods in Spain's past. It has often been called the dawn of the Spanish Renaissance. The period was one of strife: between the nobility and the King and his minister, between different powerful grandees, between old and new ideas in politics and literature. The centuries-old struggle against the Muslims, which would finally culminate in the capture of Granada at the end of the century, seemed to be in abeyance. Occasional campaigns were waged, especially in the early years of the King's reign, but the holy war of the *Reconquista* no longer held the center of the stage, and indeed had not for some time. The combative energies of the kingdom were turned to internal struggles for power. Scarcely a year can be found in which plots, schemes, open defiance of authority or diplomatic maneuvering and realignment were not going on.

In literature, too, this was a time of intense activity. The writing of history flourished, not only in royal chronicles, as in past ages, but also in accounts of private heroes and particular undertakings. Poetry abounded. Indeed, the writing of verse seems to have become a *de rigueur* accomplishment for the courtiers of Castile; the *cancionero,* or collection of verse, that Juan Alfonso de Baena prepared and presented to the King, alone contains the names of some fifty-four poets, some from the last half of the preceding century, but most from the reign of Juan II. There were also an incipient humanism and an erudite spirit that definitely foreshadow the Spanish Renaissance.

The ferment of new ideas and attitudes, the budding relations with Italy, the clash of personalities, the appearance on the scene of noble or ignoble, outstanding or eccentric characters, to say nothing of a great variety of literary expression, make this a most curious and exciting half century.

The purpose of this volume is to offer, in translation, selections from fifteenth century Castilian prose writers, in order to give English-speaking readers some idea of the life in and around the court of Juan II. It does not pretend to be either a history, sociological study or literary *précis*. It must of necessity be limited exclusively to the upper classes, for the authors of the period rarely make mention of the common people. It is hoped, however, that within such limitations, these passages will reveal to the reader various facets of life in this turbulent period, starting with a description of the country and its rulers, and continuing to political life, warfare, chivalry, such aspects of physical life as food, clothing, spectacles and amusements, and travel, the sentimental life and, finally, intellectual life.

Since this book is not intended for experts in the fields of fifteenth century Spanish history or literature, who would probably prefer to read the material in the original Castilian, an attempt will be made to orient the reader by giving some brief notes before each selection, to clarify the events or people discussed and place them in their proper setting, or to give a few facts concerning the work and author from which the excerpt is taken.

The translations, for good or bad, are my own. However, in the hope that some readers may be enticed to read those complete works that are available, I shall give in an appendix the editions of the few works used that have previously appeared in translation, in versions which I sincerely recommend. For the sake of completeness, a second appendix will list some editions of the original Spanish works.

A final word concerning the translation: normally I have preferred to give an entire chapter or section, but occasionally a passage has been omitted because it was felt to be too repetitive or not to the point. These omissions are always indicated. Proper names have been left in their Spanish originals, as have certain titles for which a single adequate English equivalent is not available, such as *adelantado* (the governor of a province), *alcaide* (governor or warden of a castle), etc. Certain technical terms are treated in notes.

TABLE OF CONTENTS

THE LAND AND THE PEOPLE

In the first half of the fifteenth century Spain was not yet unified. Besides the kingdom of Granada, the last remnant of Moorish power in the Iberian Peninsula, the Spain we know was divided into the realms of Juan II (which included the ancient kingdoms of Castile, Leon and Galicia) and the independent kingdoms of Aragon and Navarre. There is no doubt, however, that Castile was the dominant force, the holder of hegemony in the affairs of the Peninsula. It is this kingdom of Castile that Alfonso de Cartagena described with pride.

Cartagena (1385 or 86-1456), like his father don Pablo de Santa María, was Bishop of Burgos (both father and son had been converted from Judaism). He was one of the most learned and able men of Spain in his time; he translated works of Seneca, Cicero and Boccaccio to Castilian and wrote original treatises on legal, moral and literary topics. He was in contact with Italian humanists, Leonardo Bruni de Arezzo, Francesco Piccolpasso, Pietro Candido Decembri *et al.*, and Pope Eugene IV is reputed to have said that if the learned Bishop of Burgos came to his court, it would be with great confusion that he himself would sit on the throne of St. Peter. In 1434 Cartagena was named a member of the Spanish delegation to the Council of Basel. There a harsh dispute took place between the English and Castilian representatives over precedence in the Council assembly and Cartagena was given the task of speaking for Castile. Among his arguments, he brought forth his nation's antiquity, as representative of all Spain and heir to the Gothic empire in the Peninsula, its long history as a Christian nation, while England was still a pagan region, its war against the Moors to extend Christianity, its fame as the burial place of the Apostle St. James and the nobility of its cities. He also alleged the superiority of Castile over England in extent and variety of lands and people. This is the section presented here, taken from the Bishop's own Spanish translation of his Latin speech. Anecdote has it that when Cartagena finished speaking, he turned to don Juan de Silva, the royal ensign, and the knights who accompanied him, and said: "I have done my duty as a scholar; you do yours as a knight." The Castilian knights then charged the English ambassadors and cleared the seats, so the representatives of Juan II could sit in what they considered their proper place. (The fact that the Council took two years to decide in favor of Castile's claims puts some doubt on the authenticity of this story.)

Now let us see these things and treat them in two points, so as not to waste our words vainly, and let them be these: the first is the grandeur and breadth of the land and the multitude of cities, towns and villages; and this is what Aristotle says: "the multitude of lands and possession of towns." The second is a pleasing variety of lands and peoples, and this is what follows in the statement of Aristotle, who says: "diverse among themselves in multitude and grandeur and beauty."

As for the first point, to wit, the multitude of the land and possession of towns — it is clear that the kingdom of Castile, whose ruler is my lord, the King, is much greater in territory and has a greater number of cities and towns than there are in England. And this is obvious to anyone who has seen both of these kingdoms. But inasmuch as the attestations of men vary and differ at times because of their diverse preferences, let us not try to bring forth witnesses for this, but let us prove it with authentic writings.

John says in the *Catholicon* — and all those who have written on the divisions of lands — that in Spain there are six provinces, namely, that of Tarragona, that of Cartagena, Lusitania, Galicia, Betica and the gateway to the sea, in the realm of Africa. Of these, four are entirely under the dominion of my lord, the King, to wit, Cartagena, Lusitania (which is Extremadura), Betica (which is Andalusia) and Galicia, and he holds moreover the passage to the Mediterranean Sea, for he has there strong Tarifa.

And it is certain that in the length of this kingdom, which begins with Lorca — which is near Almeria, a city in the kingdom of Granada — and extends to the end of Galicia, there are thirty legal *jornadas.* [1] And in its breadth, which is from Tarifa to the town called Fuenterrabía, which is near Bayonne in Guiana, there are a good twenty-five *jornadas.* Thus one can say somewhat of the King, my lord — although to be sure, not in a general sense as applying to the whole world, as is written about our Saviour, nor with respect to that sovereign and everlasting dominion that is divine, but speaking of temporal and passing dominion — those words of the psalm: that he rules from sea to sea and from the river to the ends of the sphere and the roundness of the earth. For, from Cartagena and the kingdom of Murcia, which is near the Mediterranean Sea, to Biscay and Galicia, which are on the shores of the Ocean Sea, and from the river called the Ebro, which separates further Spain from nearer Spain, to the town which in fact is, and in name is called Finisterre, which is the very end of the west, all is subject to his royal crown ...

As for the second point, concerning the pleasing difference of peoples, the kingdom of Castile manifestly surpasses England, for under the dominion of my lord, the King, are diverse nations and diverse languages and diverse kinds of equipment for war, both on sea and on land. For the Castilians and Galicians and Basques are different nations and speak completely different languages. And for naval warfare my lord, the King, has ships and galleys. And for war on land he has men at arms provided with noble horses and very strong armor, and he also has light cavalry that use Moorish arms and pursue the enemy with marvelous agility and raid their land, and after they have destroyed and laid waste, return to the combat of the men at arms. In England there are not so many nations, nor is there such a fine difference of people. And the King of England, although he has ships, does not have galleys for sea warfare, and although he has horsemen and men at arms provided with regular armor for war on land, he does not have light cavalry. Thus there are greater power and more pleasing variety of peoples and lands under my lord, the King of Castile, than under the King of England, from which it follows that his princedom is more honorable and the dignity of his crown more lofty, and hence greater honor is due him.

---

[1] A *jornada* is the distance travelled in a day's march.

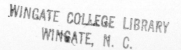

I shall not now mention the beauty and grandeur of his court, but, speaking with peace and reverence for all princes, I could say that within this part of the known world, there is not a court of any prince which, except for some bustle and agitation of war, is as frequented and full of so many prelates, counts, barons and other nobles, and of such a crowd of ordinary people as is the royal court of Castile, continuously and without exception of time.

(Alonso de Cartagena, *Discurso sobre la Precedencia del Rey Católico sobre el de Inglaterra en el Concilio de Basilea.*)

CLASSES OF PEOPLE

Some indication of the classes of society in the fifteenth century is provided by the introduction to the didactic-novelistic work *Los doze trabajos de Hércules (The twelve labors of Hercules)* by Enrique de Villena. This work, composed originally in Catalan in 1417 and translated to Castilian by the author himself, can be considered typical of the pre-Renaissance treatment of classical mythology in its fusing of Graeco-Roman fabulous material with Christian allegory —each labor of Hercules symbolizes the victory of some virtue over the opposite vice. Each of the labors, moreover, is presented in four parts: first the author retells the "story"; next is an allegorical or moral explanation of it; in third place comes a discussion of the "reality" of the events; and finally the lesson is applied to one of the classes of human society. Since the labors of Hercules were twelve in number, the author necessarily divides humanity into twelve classes. Obviously this is arbitrary, but it does offer a somewhat more detailed treatment of the ranks and hierarchies of the period than the more customary medieval separation of society, the well-known tripartition into those who pray, those who defend the land and those who work.

A more detailed introduction to Enrique de Villena will be found before the section on food.

...The world is divided into twelve main, notable classes, under which all the others are included, to wit: the class of prince, that of prelate, knight, religious, citizen, merchant, peasant, skilled

worker, teacher, pupil, recluse and woman. And each of these classes contains various different ranks; like the class of prince, which
represents emperors, kings, dukes, marquises, counts, viscounts,
captains, governors and all others who have a secular office and
jurisdiction, or are to rule over companions or family. For each
has a primacy of its kind and manner. Under the class of prelate,
I understand the Pope, cardinals, patriarchs, primates, archbishops,
bishops, abbots, priors, masters of orders, vicars, rectors, officers,
ministers, guardians, stewards and all others who have ecclesiastical office and jurisdiction, or are to rule subjects through ecclesiastical law. For each of these holds a prelature in his degree
and manner. By class of knight, I understand grandee, noble, lord,
infanzón, [1] armed knight, gentleman and all others that are noblemen to whom it pertains to use, practice and increase virtuous and
good customs, for the preservation of the common weal. By class
of religious, I understand Christians, and the degrees of specific
religious life, such as chaplains and friars, and under the name
of friars, the different orders, i.e., black monks, white monks,
Franciscans, Dominicans and others, and also women in orders;
in short, in this are included all people who live under a certain
rule or habit, community, confraternity, society or brotherhood.
By class of citizen, I understand honest citizens, burghers, ur-
banites, towns people who do not live by their work or have a
recognized occupation by which they earn a living. By class of
merchant, I understand buyers and sellers or sea-going people who,
through gains of fleets and sea voyages, set prices and make contracts by way of trade, gaining thereby certain benefit. Also included in this group are innkeepers, apothecaries, shopkeepers and
all others who, by certain prices and contracts, seek to make profits
by which they live. By class of peasant, I understand farmers, dig-
gers, tillers, horticulturists, those who hire themselves out by the
day, those who carry on their backs loads of wool and cloths and
other such cargoes from one house to another, and also fishermen,
muleteers and others who live by their physical labor, doing low
and despised jobs and occupations, such as those who cart manu-
re and clean filthy places and the like. By class of skilled worker, I

---

[1] *Infanzones* were an ancient order of noblemen.

understand carpenters, silversmiths, blacksmiths, weavers, painters and others who gain their bread working with their hands for public employment, selling the fruit of their labor. By class of teacher, I understand masters in theology, doctors of civil and canon law, teachers of medicine and the arts, philosophers, bachelors and others who know how, can and have the authority to impart any knowledge, science, art, doctrine or instruction to pupils. By class of pupil, I understand students, servants at schools, repeaters and all others who, under the training of a teacher, gain instruction, or are preparing to gain it, in a scientific or moral manner. By class of recluse, I understand hermits, anchorites, isolated or secluded persons, forest dwellers and all others who live removed from companionship, devoting themselves to the contemplative life. By class of woman, I understand duenna, maiden, girl, married woman, widow, servant girl, child and all other feminine or womanly degrees, in whatever high or subordinate position they may be found. Of the people who live outside of these classes named and their ways, such as pirates or corsairs, thieves, robbers, housebreakers, arsonists, vagabonds, wanderers, vagrants, infidels, pagans and the like, I make no mention, for, proscribed or cast out of virtuous and licit life, they form no class by themselves, nor are they healthy members of the universal mystic body of the human race and congregation of the world.

(Enrique de Villena, Introduction to *Los doze trabajos de Hércules.*)

THE RULERS

The use of the plural, "rulers," to head this section is deliberate. Although Juan II become King of Castile and Leon at the age of twenty-two months, and supposedly assumed personal direction of his government after a regency of fourteen years, it is doubtful that he was ever more than king in name. He was a weak monarch; he seems to have been a person of charm and ability, interested in literature and the arts, which he actively fomented, but he had no taste for government. His reign was characterized by the constant anarchy of the nobles, including the rulers of Aragon and Navarre who, as grandees of Castile, meddled in her affairs and often led the attempts to depose his Constable. Given his evident inability or disinclination to rule, perhaps the King's most successful move was to entrust his affairs to don Álvaro de Luna. This famous Constable of Castile, Grand Master of the Order of Santiago and favorite of the King was the power at court for the most part of thirty-five years. He was the most hated man of his time, undoubtedly because of his very ability to frustrate the designs of the fractious nobles. Just the opposite of the King in this respect, he had the desire to govern and the energy to work at it. He finally fell before the impact of his enemies, who had tried for years to get rid of him, and was executed in 1453, one year before the King himself died. One of the ironies of his life was that the second wife of Juan II, doña Isabel of Portugal, with whom he had urged the King to form a marital alliance, turned out to be one of his most bitter enemies. Don Alvaro's name will appear often, throughout this collection.

The portrayals of King and Constable here presented are from the *Generaciones y semblanzas (Lineages and biographies)* of Fernán Pérez de Guzmán (1376-1460). A nephew of one famous writer, the poet and historian Pero López de Ayala, and uncle to another, the Marquis of

Santillana (see below, the section on literary activity), Pérez de Guzmán is often considered the finest prose writer of the period. After an active career in military, political and court life, he retired at the age of fity-six to his estates at Batres, where he dedicated himself to study and writing. He was a friend of Alonso de Cartagena, with whom he maintained a correspondence. His *Generaciones y semblanzas* are a collection, with a prologue, of thirty-six brief biographical sketches of notable people in the reigns of King Enrique III and his son, Juan II, and were written about 1450. The portraits of Juan II and don Álvaro de Luna were not added until five years later, after both had died. The biographies are noted for their objectivity, psychological analysis and temperate judgments.

JUAN II OF CASTILE

Don Juan, the second of the kings who bore this name in Castile, was the son of King Enrique III and his wife, Queen Catalina. He was born in Toro on Friday, the sixth of March, the day of St. Thomas, in the year of our Lord 1405, and he began to reign on Christmas Day, 1407, for his father, the King, died in the city of Toledo on that day. Thus he was proclaimed King when he was twenty-two months old, there being present Prince Fernando, his uncle, don Ruy López Dávalos, the Constable of Castile, Juan de Velasco, chief chamberlain of the King, Diego López Destúñiga, his Chief Justice, don Sancho de Rojas, Bishop of Palencia, who was afterwards Archbishop of Toledo, and don Juan de Illescas, Bishop of Sigüenza. At the time his father died, he was in Segovia, where his mother, the Queen, kept him. According to the will of the King, his regents and guardians were the Queen and the Prince, and the custody and care of the child King was given to Diego López Destúñiga and Juan de Velasco, but because the Queen felt very offended by that, and also because it did not please the grandees of the realm, they were indemnified and the Queen kept possession of the King. A few days after the King, his father, died, the Prince and all the knights who were with him left Toledo for Segovia, where the King was, and many great prelates and knights and the law officers of the cities and towns came, so there was a great gathering of people. Certain arguments took place between the

Queen and the Prince as to the form of the regency, but it was agreed on in this manner: that the Queen should have the government on the other side of the passes in the direction of Burgos, along with Cordoba and some other places that belonged to her administration, and the Prince had the part on this side of the passes, toward Toledo and Andalusia, along with Burgos and other places. When this was settled, the Prince set out for the war against the Moors, and with him went all the grandees of the kingdom, and the Queen remained in Segovia with the King. What the Prince did that year and the following in that war, since it has previously been told, will not be repeated here, but I shall only say that, if the sins of Castile had not provoked our Lord to indignation, so that there should be some hindrance to it, doubtlessly this noble Prince would have put an end to that war and would have restored to Spain her former territory, throwing out the Moors and returning it to the Christians. But while this Prince was besieging Antequera, having won one battle and keeping the Moors hard pressed, King Martin of Aragon died without children and the kingdom rightfully went to Prince don Fernando, who was the son of Queen Leonor of Castile, the sister of King Martin, and for that reason the Prince had to abandon the aforementioned war and turn to the pursuit of the Kingdom of Aragon. This was a great loss for Castile, both because that conquest was lost and because the Prince withdrew from the government of the realm, which he had been ruling in such peace as, I swear, became evident later, in the great misfortunes and evils that have come about through lack of good government, for good is never recognized except through its opposite.

Turning again to this King Juan, one should know that he was tall and large-limbed, but not of good figure nor great strength; a good visage, fair and blond, high-shouldered, a large face, slightly precipitate in talking, calm and gentle, very moderate and unaffected in his speech. And because his nature was strange and wondrous, I must deal with it at some length. The fact was that he was a man who spoke discreetly and reasonably and he had a knowledge of men, to understand which one spoke better, more prudently and pleasingly. He liked to listen to sagacious and accomplished people and he took careful note of what he heard from them. He could speak and understand Latin, he read very well and liked books and histories, he willingly listened to poetic compositions and knew their artifices, he took pleasure in hearing happy and well chosen words and he himself could use them well. He took great part in the hunt and chase and understood all about it. He knew the art of music and sang and played well, and he even comported himself well in jousting and equestrian exercises. But even though he had a fair share of all these accomplishments, in those that are truly virtues and are necessary to every man, especially to kings, he was very deficient. For the principal virtue of a king, after religious faith, is to be industrious and diligent in the governing and administration of his kingdom, as is proved by that wisest of kings, Solomon, who, being commanded by God to seek whatever he desired, asked only for wisdom to rule and govern his people, and this request was so agreeable to our Lord that He granted him that and other singular accomplishments. Now this King was so deficient and lacking in this virtue that, having all the aforementioned graces, never for a single hour would he attend to or work on the administration of the realm, although there took place in Castile in his time as many uprisings and agitations and misfortunes and dangers as there had been in the times of kings past for over two hundred years, from which there came considerable danger to his person and reputation. So great was his negligence and remissness in the governing of the realm, while he devoted himself to other tasks, more pleasurable and delightful than useful or honorable, that he never paid any attention to it. And although one can find in those histories that he read the misfortunes and harm that befell kings and their kingdoms through the negligence and remissness of the rulers and, also, although many great prelates and knights told him that his person and realm were in great danger because of his inattention to the government of his kingdom and that his reputation was impaired thereby and, what was more serious, that his conscience was heavily burdened and he would have to account very strictly to God for the evil that came to his subjects through the deficiency of his rule, since God had given him discretion and intelligence to attend to it —with all this, even though he himself could see the disobedience that was shown him and how irreverently he was treated and the inattention that was paid his letters and commands— with all this, never for a single day did he turn his face to nor exert his mind on the order-

ing of his household or the governing of his kingdom, but left the
management of it all to his Constable, in whom he placed such
great and extraordinary trust that, to those who did not see it, it
would seem an incredible thing, and to those who did see it, it was
a strange and wondrous influence. For whether it concerned his rents
and treasures, or the operation of his household, or the justice of
his realm, not only was everything done by the Constable's command, but without his orders nothing was done, for even though
the decrees and letters of justice, warrants, favors and royal grants
were made in the name of the King and signed with his name,
neither did the secretaries write, not the King sign, nor the chancellor seal, nor did the letters have validity or execution without the
will of the Constable. So great and singular was the trust that
the King placed in the Constable, and so great and excessive his
power, that it is hard to know of any king or prince, however feared
and obeyed he might be in his realm, who was more feared and
obeyed than was don Álvaro de Luna in Castile, nor who governed and administered with greater freedom of action. For not only
in positions, ranks and favors that the King could confer, but in
ecclesiastical dignities and benefices, there was no one in the kingdom who dared seek them from the Pope, or even accept his
writ, if *proprio motu* he did so without the consent of the Constable. Thus everything temporal and spiritual was in his power. All
the authority of the King was in signing the letters, but their dis-
position and execution depended on the Constable. His power
extended so much and the efficacy of the King shrank to such a
degree that, from the greatest office in the kingdom to the smallest
favor, very few people came to ask or thank the King, but sought
it from the Constable and thanked him for it. Even more astonish-
ing to relate and hear is that even in his natural acts he was so
much under the control of the Constable that, although he was
young and of good constitution and had a young and beautiful
wife for his Queen, if the Constable gainsaid it, he would not go
to sleep in her room, nor amuse himself with other women, although
by nature he was favorably disposed toward them. In conclusion:
two very amazing points are to be noted here; the first is that a
king of reasonable understanding in many things could be completely remiss and negligent in the governing of his realm, being
moved to it neither by discretion nor by the experience of many

hardships that he underwent in the upheavals and revolts that occurred in his kingdom, nor by the admonitions and warnings of
great knights and churchmen who spoke to him about it. What
is more, his natural inclination could not have such strength and
vigor, but that he should completely and without limit place himself under the control and advice of the Constable with more
obedience than ever a humble child paid his father or a dutiful
monk his abbot or prior. There were some people who, seeing this
special love and excessive trust, thought it was due to bewitch-
ment and the black arts, but there was nothing certain in this,
even though some investigations were made concerning it. The
second point is that a knight without relatives and with such poor
beginnings, in such a great kingdom where there were so many
powerful knights, and in a time of a king who was so little obeyed
and feared, could have such extraordinary power. For, although we
might wish to say that this was by virtue of the King, how could
he who did not have power for himself give it to another? Or
how can the lieutenant be obeyed when he who puts him in his
place does not find obedience? In truth, I doubt that one could
give a clear explanation for this, unless He who made the King's
nature so strange should give it, for He can explain the power of
the Constable. For myself, I do not know which of these two things
is more to be marvelled at, the nature of the King or the power of
the Constable.

In the time of this King Juan, there took place in Castile many
events, outstanding and strange rather than good or worthy of
memory or useful and advantageous to the realm. For as soon as
his uncle, King Fernando of Aragon, left this life, so did peace
and harmony leave Castile. Also, when Queen Catalina, the mother
of the King, died, Prince Enrique, the Master of Santiago, don
Sancho de Rojas, Archbishop of Toledo, don Alfonso Enríquez,
Admiral of Castile, don Ruy López Dávalos, Constable, Juan de
Velasco, lord chamberlain of the King, and Pedro Manrique, chief
adelantado of Castile, and many other grandees of the kingdom
gathered in Valladolid and, by the agreement and consent of all,
brought the King out of that house (which is near St. Paul's) in
which his mother, the Queen, had kept him for more than six years,
during which time he did not go out, fearing that he would be seized. Thus the day he left there seemed like a second birth for him,

for just as on the day he was born he came into the light of this life, so on the day he left that lodging did he see his kingdom and know his people, for previously he knew only the guards who were there with him and a few knights, when they came to pay him homage. When he left there, they took him to Tordesillas, and the principal men who were ruling the kingdom were don Sancho de Rojas, the Admiral don Alfonso Enríquez, the Constable Ruy López Dávalos and the *adelantado* Pedro Manrique. For although the Princes Juan and Enrique, the sons of King Fernando of Aragon, were there, they were very young and afflicted by that royal ailment that is common and general to all royal youths, in that they were ruled and governed by tutors and masters (and there are some who never get over this ailment). Other great lords were there, too, but all actions were carried out by these four. From Tordesillas they went to Medina del Campo, where the King was betrothed to Princess María, the daughter of King Fernando of Aragon, and from there the King went to Madrid, where he took over the government of his realms, for he had reached the age of fourteen. Great festivities and ceremonies were held, for all the grandees and law officers of the kindom came. And although the administration of the kingdom was handed over to him there, since he followed his natural temperament and that almost monstrous remissness and negligence, the whole time he reigned might better be called tutelage, rather than royal rule or administration. Thus he held the royal title and name —I won't say acts or deeds of king— for almost forty-seven years, from the day his father died in Toledo to the day he died in Valladolid, during which time he never had the appearance or aspect of king, but was always controlled and governed. For even after the death of his Constable, don Alvaro de Luna, whom he survived a little more than a year, he was controlled and governed by don Lope de Barrientos, the Bishop of Cuenca, and Fray Gonzalo de Illescas, the Prior of Guadalupe, and some other men of low origin and little worth; and if, after the death of the Constable, he showed some vigor and will, it was only in his greed to amass treasures, to which he willingly devoted himself, but not in ruling his realms or restoring and repairing the wrongs and misfortunes that befell them in the forty-seven years that he held the name and title of king. While he was in Valladolid, he fell ill with the double ague, which lasted many days, and according to hearsay, he conducted himself very badly, for he was very fond of eating and unrestrained. Although he recovered from the ague, he was left indisposed and, continuing his poor regimen, had first some very serious attacks and then died in Valladolid, the twenty-second of July, 1454, and was buried in the monastery of Miraflores, where he had established Carthusian friars.

A little more than a year before this King Juan died, contrary to the expectations of everyone —pricked and stimulated, as it is thought, by the will of God, or because his Constable kept him more under his power and constrained than ever and did not give him a chance to do anything he wished, for he was always surrounded by people in the Constable's service, without whom he could do or say nothing, and it is even said that the service and maintenance of his table were so poor and mean that it caused everyone to talk, nor did he allow him to be with or enjoy his second wife, the Queen, when he wanted: whether this was the cause or, as is more believable, the greed of the Amorite was now fulfilled (as St. Augustine puts it) and divine justice could not and would not tolerate his tyranny and usurpation of power— while the King was in Burgos, the Constable heard that Alonso Pérez de Vivero, whom he had raised up out of the dirt and made a great lord and given great influence with the King, was plotting his downfall and destruction with the King, and, not being able to be forbearing in the matter, he had him come to his home on Good Friday, an inopportune day for such an act, and had him killed. Immediately afterward, on Wednesday of Easter week, it being the will of our Lord to do a new work, the day that should have been a resurrection was the passion of this Constable. To the great surprise and almost disbelief of the entire kingdom, the King ordered don Alvaro de Stúñiga, who was afterwards Count of Plasencia, to arrest him. He seized whatever he found on him and, leaving Burgos, took him to Valladolid and had him placed in irons, in a wooden cage, in Portillo. What can we say here, except that we should fear and obey the obscure judgments of God! That a King, who for forty-seven years was under the control of this Constable with such exceeding patience and obedience that he did not even give the slightest sign of opposing him, should now, suddenly and with such great rigor, have him arrested and put in chains! It should even be noted that those royal Princes, the King of Navarre and Prince Enrique, with the agreement and help of all the grandees of the realm, often tried to separate him from the King and destroy him, and not only did they not succeed, but all or most of them were ruined in the attempt, perchance because they were motivated by self interest, and not by good intentions. If we wish to say that the King did this deed, it seems just the contrary, because after the Constable was dead, the King remained in that same remissness and negligence as before, nor did he do any act of vigor or courage in which he appeared to be more of a man than before. Thus it remains, that we must believe this to be the work of God alone, for as Scripture tells us, He alone works great marvels.

Getting back to the subject matter, while the Constable remained in Portillo, the King went to Escalona to seize the town and the treasure that was there. While he was in that region, because of certain information he had and proceeding as in a manifest case, with the advice of the counselors who were at his court, he pronounced sentence that don Alvaro should be beheaded, and he was taken from Portillo to Valladolid and there, publicly and like a common criminal, he was beheaded. According to reports, he prepared to meet his death more bravely than devoutly, for the things he did and the words he said that day concerned reputation rather than devotion.

As for this King Juan, in the opinion of some who knew him, he was by nature greedy and lustful and even vindictive, but he lacked the will to carry it out. The strange ways and nature of this King and the evils that came to his realms through them are attributed, in the judgment of many, to the sins of the inhabitants of this kingdom, in accordance with Holy Scripture, which says: "because of the sins of the people God makes the hypocrite to reign." Truly, whoever knew and considered him well will see that such a King's condition and so many evils that followed therefrom were due to the great sins of the people.

At his death, this King left his son, Prince Enrique, who is now reigning, and Prince Alfonso and Princess Isabel.

(Fernán Pérez de Guzmán, *Generaciones y semblanzas*.)

Don Alvaro de Luna

Don Alvaro de Luna, Master of the Order of Santiago and Constable of Castile, was the illegitimate son of Alvaro de Luna, a good and noble knight. This house of Luna is one of the greatest in the Kingdom of Aragon, and has had very notable people, both knights and clergymen, among whom flourished that venerable and sagacious apostolic father, Pedro de Luna, called Pope Benedict the Thirteenth. And all of this house of Luna greatly served the Kingdom of Castile. When the father of this Constable died, the small child was left in quite a low and poor condition, and for a while his uncle, don Pedro de Luna, who was Archbishop of Toledo, reared him. When he died, the very young boy was left in the household of the aforementioned King Juan, who had for him that excessive and wondrous fondness that has already been mentioned.

One should know that this Constable had a small body and tiny face, but he was well formed of limb, of good strength and a very good rider, quite skilled in arms and expert in tourneys, very pleasing and well spoken in the palace, even though he was somewhat hesitant in his speech, very discreet, a great dissembler, feigner and cautious, and one who took much pleasure in using such arts and precautions, so that it seemed to come to him naturally. He was considered valiant, although he did not have great occasion to show it in arms, but on those occasions which befell him he displayed good courage. In the disputes and altercations of the palace (which is another way of being courageous) he showed himself to be a man of spirit and valor. He boasted a great deal about lineage, forgetting his mother's low and humble origins. He was brave and daring enough to accept and use the great power he sought, for, either because he had it for a long time and it became natural to him or because his fortune and presumption were so great, he enjoyed more the power of king than of knight. It cannot be denied that he had enough skills as far as the things of the world are concerned, for he liked very much to discuss his affairs with discreet men and he rewarded with deeds the good advice they gave him. He helped many people with the King and through him they obtained favors and great benefits from the King, and if he harmed many, he also forgave many the grave errors they committed against him. He was inordinately greedy for vassals and treasures, so much so that, just as hydropics never lose their thirst, he never lost his desire to gain and possess, his insatiable greed never being satisfied, for on the very day that the King gave him, or rather he took, a large town, he would take over one of the King's lances, if the post became vacant. Thus, while desiring the great, he did not disdain the little. It would be difficult to relate his great greed, for being left at the death of his father poor and destitute, on the day he died he possessed more than 20,000 vassals, without counting the Mastership of Santiago, the many offices of the King, and the great quantities of *maravedis* on his books. It is thought that his income amounted to nearly 100,000 *doblas,* without the duties which came to him from the King and from the offices of treasurers and taxgatherers, which were many and varied. So great was the fire of his insatiable greed that each day he seemed only to be beginning to amass wealth. He acquired such treasures that, although the exact figure could not be known because his imprisonment and death occurred as they did, judging by what he earned and kept, it was the common opinion that he alone had more wealth than all the great men and prelates of Spain. He had to have whatever town or possession was near his, either through exchange or purchase, and thus his patrimony spread and increased like the plague, which infects whatever is near it. In this way he obtained holdings and possessions from religious orders and churches, by exchanges or sales that no one dared oppose, and everything he gave for the sales and exchanges was paid for by the King. He had many dignities of the Church go to his relatives, not taking into consideration their unworthiness or inadequacy. Thus he obtained for one of his brothers the church of Seville and later that of Toledo, and for one of his young nephews, the church of Santiago, for the Pope did not refuse any petition of his. Who could say how far his greed and power extended! For, of the thirty-two years that he ruled and governed the kingdom, in twenty of them no appointment, either in temporal or spiritual matters, was made except by his hand and with his consent. It cannot be denied that he helped and did much good for many people, in some of whom he found little gratitude. In only this and in his children was fortune contrary to him, for he found in some people little gratitude and he had a son who was very unwise. Well, if he was so greedy for towns and vassals and wealth, no less was his ambition

for honors and preeminence, for he did not let go of the smallest
part of anything he was able to get. To a friend of his who wrote
him in a letter that he ought to be more moderate in his acquisitions,
he replied with that evangelical authority: *Qui venerit ad me non
ejiciam foras,* which means, "What comes to me I will not reject,"
although when our Lord said this, he did not say it for such a
purpose. His diligence and care in keeping and preserving his power
and favor with the King were such that it seemed he left nothing
to God to do, for as soon as the King showed the slightest good
will toward anyone, that person was immediately ejected, and he did
not allow anyone to be near the King except those whom he greatly
trusted.

This Constable was by nature very suspicious, and suspicion
increased in him with cause, because many were envious of him
and desired to take his place, and thus, with such suspicions and
fears, he easily believed whatever was told him, and he was not
lacking tale-bearers, for flatterers and tale-bearers are common to
great men. And with this he made the King carry out many sentences
of imprisonment and banishment, confiscations of property and
deaths, for which he found enough acceptance, for by dividing among
some what he took from others he had sufficient helpers, for the
laudable custom of the Castilians has reached such a point that they
would consent to have a relative or friend arrested and killed, to have
the spoils. But because there were some deaths in these sentences
that the King carried out at his advice, I do not wish to lie or assign
him blame which he did not deserve, for I have heard it said by
some people, who were in a position to know if they wanted to tell
the truth, that he prevented some deaths that the King, who was
naturally cruel and vindictive, wanted to commit, and I would be
willing to believe this opinion.

In his time there were great and terrible losses, not only in
property and person, but what is more to be regretted and lamented,
in the exercise and use of virtues and honesty. With greed to acquire
wealth and, on the other hand, with rancor and vengeance against
one another, all shame and honesty put aside, they gave free rein
to great vices, for from this were born deceptions, malice, falsehood, craftiness, false oaths and contracts, and many other diverse
cunning devices and tricks, so that the greatest deceptions and

Suero de Quiñones were seized; don Manrique, the brother of the Admiral don Fadrique, was twice arrested, and this Admiral don Fadrique and the Count of Castro were exiled; Garci Sánchez Alvarado was executed; and the noble Princes, the King of Navarre and Prince Enrique were banished a second time and their patrimony again divided. Who could relate the sad and dolorous trial of unfortunate Spain and the evils that befell her! In the judgment of many this has come about because of the sins of her inhabitants, and only secondarily because of the remiss and negligent condition of the King and the greed and unbridled ambition of the Constable, placing some of the blame on the great lords and knights, while not denying that, as we can find in histories, Spain was always fickle and unstable in her deeds and scarcely ever lacked affronts and scandals. But there was never a time that lasted as long as this, which continued for forty years, nor was there a king who thus let himself be ruled and governed all his life, nor a favorite who gained such excessive power and lasted so long. There were some people who, either maliciously or unthinkingly, wished to defame the King of Navarre and Prince Enrique and, with them, the Admiral and the Count of Castro, the Count of Benavente and the *adelantado* Pero Manrique and many others who followed their opinion, and said that they were plotting the King's death and the usurpation of the realm, which was undoubtedly malice and falsehood. Leaving aside words and turning to experience, which often shows the truth of the matter, —it is known by everyone that when, at Tordesillas, Prince Enrique, the Constable Ruy López, Garci Fernández Manrique, Count of Castañeda, and the *adelantado* Pero Manrique entered the King's palace (which was the first affront of that time) and seized the palace and removed Juan Hurtado de Mendoza, chief steward of the King, who was at that time very close to him, and left there Alvaro de Luna, who was afterwards Constable, and were with the King more than seven months, if they wanted to commit any knavery they had every opportunity to do so, but just the opposite appeared, for they left the said Alvaro de Luna there to please the King, and His Majesty was married in Avila and was always respected as their King and natural lord. Afterwards, when the King of Navarre, the Prince and all the grandees of the realm gathered in Valladolid and decreed that the Constable should leave the court, the King was in their power almost a year and it they had wanted to commit any disloyalty against him they had quite enough power and freedom to do so, but the opposite appeared in their deeds, for they still paid him that respect and reverence which they ought, and did him every service and pleasure they could. It is true that they did not please or satisfy him, because he was separated from the Constable. Some time later, at Castronuño, when the above named King and Prince, the *adelantado* Pero Manrique, the Marquis of Santillana, the Admiral, Gutierre de Toledo, the Archbishop of Seville, the Count of Benavente, the Count of Plazencia and other great lords, and the Count of Haro forced the Constable to leave the court, the King remained in their power more than a year, being served and treated as King. Similarly, in Medina del Campo, which was the greatest and most serious affront committed until that time, the city being forceably entered with the greatest rigor and armed scandal, the King was always protected and treated with all humble reverence. At such a time, when men at arms are usually most proud and rash, they kissed his hand and honored him with the respect they owed him, and never did any danger ensue to him from that harsh act. Later, at Romaga near Madrigal, when the King of Navarre and the Admiral, and the Count of Benavente (with the authority of Prince Enrique, who afterwards ruled) arrested Alfonso Pérez de Vivero, chief paymaster of the King, and again seized the palace and were with the King for a year in Tordesillas, still the honor and person of the King were protected. True, he considered all that an offence and danger to his person and estate, since he could not be with the Constable. Thus the entire difference of opinion was this: the King said he wanted his person to be free, and the King of Navarre and the Prince and the grandees who followed their opinion said that they wanted the freedom of his person together with the freedom of his will, which was oppressed and subject to the Constable, and that if he showed himself free of the oppression of his will and, as King and lord, were equal to all, they would be happy to withdraw from him, but the King said his will would be free if they would leave him. And so, in this difference of opinion, the kingdom was harassed and wasted. But in all these times, it could not truthfully be said that there was any danger to the King's person, either in deed or word. The truth is this, all other opinions notwithstanding; the Princes and the grandees who followed them said that they were acting to free the King's will from the power of the Constable so that he, with good advice and by himself, might rule and govern the kingdom, and that they were acting out of love for the nation and for the common good and benefit, but, excepting his Highness, their ultimate aim was to possess and take over the position of the Constable and, seeing that the King was of a nature more to be ruled than to rule, they thought that whoever gained possession of him would rule him and, consequently, the kingdom, and they would be able to increase their estates and houses. For they knew that they could not do it as long as the Constable was there, and they endeavored to remove him. To this was added the rancor and enmities that some of the grandees had for others, and they carried on these affronts to prevail over them and to do them harm. And because they did not have good intentions nor was their aim service to God or King, or love of country, they did not succeed in their efforts, but wasted and destroyed the kingdom with such affronts and commotions, and many perished, as has been said. For, although the judgments of our Lord are secret and obscure to us and very often seem to go against reason since we do not comprehend them, whoever will diligently try to understand and meditate upon them will indeed see that great undertakings and deeds never have a good end without good and righteous intentions. And so, I would indeed excuse these Princes and the great knights who followed and advised them, of disloyalty or tyranny to the person of the King and to his crown, believing that they were never lacking in respect for it, but I would not dare excuse them for their erroneous methods and unjust intentions, for which I believe they failed in all their proceedings, not only not carrying them out, but being destroyed in them, while innocent and guiltless people suffered along with them. Nor shall I be silent or consent to the opinion that some people ignorantly or simple-mindedly hold, and that some preach and publicize for their own benefit, saying that they followed the opinion of the Constable and the will of the King only through zealous loyalty and love. I do not say, nor please it God that I should say, to the injury of so many noble and great men, that they were not loyal and respectful to the King, but I do say that this loyalty was involved and mingled with great interests, so much so that I believe that if someone had removed those interests and if those who followed the King had not been thrown the spoils of others, they might have been benevolent mediators and judges, rather than the harsh executioners that they were. And thus I conclude that, as far as the truth is concerned, some may have had a more plausible and fine appearance of reason, but the main intention was entirely to profit, so that it could be said, in pure truth, that neither side in this controversy, neither plaintiffs nor defendants, were in the right, but some had a fairer reputation and more plausible and legal or legitimate cause than others. But with regard to guarding the King's person and preserving him and the crown, I swear to God that I never heard or knew of any disrespect.

To speak plainly and truthfully of the battle of Olmedo, which was the last and most criminal act, I cannot judge because I was not there, nor can I very well clear them on the word of others, for events had reached such extremes that it was a question of people losing their positions, which is a case in which justice and loyalty often bungle and fail, and few persons are found in whom truth and loyalty remain absolute. In this, only King David had the most singular praise and glory, for although he was cruelly persecuted by King Saul, he refused to touch him on two occasions when he might have killed him. I do not think I have read of any other person having practiced this virtue so perfectly. As it says in the *Decretum,* "the privilege of a few does not make a common law," and so a single act is not a general rule; for one thing, because of the extreme danger to person and position in which they were, and because they did in fact move in ordered battle ranks to go against the King, I cannot judge their intentions, but the indications and appearances were not good, although it might be that if they had won the battle, avenging themselves on the others, they would have protected the King as they did at other times. But it is not for me to determine this, for, as I have said, to act with absolute loyalty in such extreme danger would be great perfection. For one can read in the Book of Kings that when those two constables of David and the house of Saul, Joab and Abner, had their encounter near the lake of Gibeon and Abner was defeated, he, seeing how Joab was pursuing him, turned to him and said: "Knowest thou not that it will be bitterness in the end? How long shall it be then, ere thou bid the people return from following their brethren?" Then Joab ceased pursuing them more, even though Abner in that battle had killed a brother of his, a good knight. However, one can think (if we wish to conjecture, choosing the best side, and even past deeds) that if these lords had won the victory, they would have protected the person of the King, as they had done other times. But this I give as my opinion, not as a determined fact. Still, I do not wish to excuse them of two charges; one, that the first and original agitation was caused by self-interest, ambition and greed, and not to give good order and rule to the kingdom; the other, that in their deeds, the method was perverted and made erroneous by scandals and hardships, which very often harms the cause. Thus, I shall give my opinion in conclusion: the cause of all these evils, both in having a remiss and negligent King, and in one knight having such daring and presumption to rule and govern such great realms and domains, not omitting the greed of the great knights, were the sins of the Spaniards.

Since our sins, which are the cause of this, do not cease and are not corrected, but rather, it is said, increase and worsen, both in quality and quantity, may it please our Lord that the punishment not increase with the sins, but through His infinite pity and mercy, with His holy mother interceding, may His sentence be mitigated and softened, giving us such devout people that we will deserve to have good kings. For my rude and humble opinion is that neither worldly goods nor prosperity are so beneficent and necessary to the kingdom as is a just and wise king, for he is a prince of peace, and our Lord, when He departed this world, left us in His last will and testament nothing other than peace. And this can be given by the good king, who has his place from God, and not by the world, as the Church sings: *"Quam mundus dare non potest."*

(Fernán Pérez de Guzmán, *Generaciones y semblanzas.*)

POLITICAL LIFE

THE MURDER OF ALONSO PÉREZ

To represent the political activities in the period of Juan II, I have chosen two major and related events from the closing years of his reign, both taken from the *Crónica de don Alvaro de Luna*. Many other passages might have been picked, either from this or other works, but I have preferred these because of the magnitude of the deeds involved. Concerning this chronicle, its erudite modern editor, Juan de Mata Carriazo, has established that the author was most probably a certain Gonzalo Chacón, who figures prominently in the relation of events. Chacón was a faithful retainer of the Constable's in his youth and later enjoyed the esteem of the Catholic Monarchs. His work was begun during the lifetime of don Alvaro, but was probably not completed until some time during the reign of Isabel and Fernando. The first printed version of the chronicle appeared in 1546, in Milan, Italy, where a great grandson and namesake of don Alvaro de Luna had it printed.

This is undoubtedly the best private chronicle of the period, unsurpassed in its animation and dramatic intensity. The style is more sophisticated than that of any other contemporary historical writing. The author relied, for the most part, on his own observation and on oral tradition, although he was a person of learning, as his references to various classical writers and, especially, the Bible show. Chacón may make mistakes of fact, but, as can be seen in his account of the death of Alonso Pérez de Vivero, he does not try to hide those things unfavorable to his hero. He does try to justify them, and finds himself hard pressed at times to do so. The chronicle is characterized by strong and sincere emotion, warmth of admiration for the hero

and indignation against his enemies, an indignation that
does not spare even the King.

The first event related here is an account of the assassin-
ation of Alonso Pérez de Vivero, a political murder plotted
and caused to be carried out by the Constable himself,
occasioned perhaps by a growing sense of frustration and
panic as he saw his enemies closing in on him. It took place
on Good Friday in the year 1453, and was a tactical error,
for it hastened don Alvaro's downfall. Chacón's account
gains vividness through the direct quoting of the speeches
of the participants and a detailed treatment not only of
events, but of motives. Of the people involved, Alonso
Pérez was the royal paymaster, the Bishop of Burgos was
Alonso de Cartagena (author of the description of the country given above), Fernando de Ribadeneyra was the chamberlain of don Alvaro, and Juan de Luna was a nephew
of the Constable's, married to his natural daughter.

How the valiant Grand Master, after due consideration,
resolved to have the traitor Alonso Pérez killed, and
concerning other things that occurred before that.

We have already written the words and admonitions that the
courageous Grand Master had given Alonso Pérez and the excuse
the latter made on that occasion. After that, with an almost super-
abundance of goodness, and to reform him completely and dissuade
him from evil, and also to make sure of him —after he had set up
the best precautions imaginable, both in establishing in different
places people he knew to be reliable, with a view to being informed
of events as they happened, and in setting up guards so that no
people could enter the castle in Burgos without his knowing it—,
since it was Lent at that time, and already Holy Week, the good
Grand Master made every effort and used every means he could
to get Alonso Pérez to go to confession, thinking that confession
would dissuade him completely from the horrible and wicked road
he was travelling and would get him out of the mire of evil into
which he was sunken and wallowing.

Therefore, he had Fernando de Ribadeneyra speak to him about
it and attract him to it in every way he could, telling him that they
should go together to one of the monasteries of that city, where there
were many fathers confessors. But just as dogs that are afflicted
with rabies abhor water and flee from the very thing that would

be a cure fo their illness, so did the traitor Alonso Pérez, as one who was afflicted with a diabolic and rabid treachery that spread throughout his veins, abhor the water and purity of the holy sacrament of confession and penance, which cleanses and washes away sin.

The fact is, Fernando de Ribadeneyra was never able to get him to go to confession; rather did he reply, after saying many other things, "that never at such a season had he felt so little contrition and so little inclination to go to confession as he did then."

Oh marvelous Redeemer of the world and true God, Jesus! Certainly Your words cannot fail! For You said, as the Holy Gospel testifies, "that the evildoer abhors the light." This certainly appeared proven and experienced in Alonso Pérez, who refused to bring to light and make manifest his horrible wickedness, even before the confessor. The good Grand Master, when he saw the obstinacy of Alonso Pérez, as Fernando de Ribadeneyra told it to him, was henceforth more suspicious of him and trusted him very little, and put him in charge of very few things, although the traitor still came twice a day to the Grand Master's lodging, to be and speak with him.

The latter, as a severe and virtuous officer against the wicked and a capital foe to them, pondered about giving that perverse, evil servant and completely treacherous and villainous knave the punishment he deserved. And the deed was arranged in the manner we shall now relate.

Our history has already mentioned how, when the Grand Master was in Tordesillas in past days, and almost at the very beginning, when he first learned of the great enmity and the enormity of the deed in which this great traitor Alonso Pérez was becoming involved, there was in the house in which the Grand Master was staying, in that city of Tordesillas, a high tower, and the Grand Master had once cleverly arranged to have his evil servant, Alonso Pérez de Vivero, thrown down from it. He had arranged it in such a way that the King would not be angered against him because of his death, but would think that Alonso Pérez had fallen from the tower through some unavoidable misfortune or chance accident.

But then, as has previously been written, the virtuous Grand Master, overcome by his own virtue, failed to put it into execution, hoping that the traitor would withdraw from that path he was travelling and would change his ways. To be sure, it would perhaps have been much better to put an end to his life in Tordesillas, so his baneful poison could not spread and infect more than it had. Yet, although the deed was not carried out then it seemed, as experience demonstrated, that the invention for killing the traitor in that way was henceforth fixed in the Grand Master's heart.

Now that the time had come when this invention was to take place, as it did take place, since there was in the Grand Master's dwelling in Burgos a tower very similar to the one in Tordesillas (so that one might well say that the material was prepared of itself to receive form), the good Grand Master was able to find a cunning, ingenious and secret way of having a section of the tower railing, from one post to another, unfastened, without anyone being able to tell it was loosened, so that if someone leaned against it, both the railing and the person leaning against it would easily fall off the tower, Thus was the deed devised and contrived; and so that no one else would run a risk going up to that tower, and also so that no one else could know the secret, except the person to whom the Grand Master had revealed it, he took personal custody of the key to the tower until the time came when the punishment of that traitor should be carried out. To be sure, the Grand Master was spurred on to it no little by an occurrence that the history will now relate.

Concerning the death of Alonso Pérez and some things that happened before that.

It was Good Friday, when every faithful Christian should prepare and reconcile himself with God and repent his sins. Thus, the noble Grand Master, his disloyal and wicked servant, Alonso Pérez, and Fernando de Ribadeneyra went this day, with clothing disguised and faces covered, to walk the stations of the Cross, as they had been wont to do in other years. After they had walked the stations, they went to the Cathedral, where the King already was, within his curtained pew before the altar, hearing the sermon for the day, which had already begun. A friar of the Order of St. Paul, who, to be sure, seemed more worldly than religious in his appearance, was preaching it.

After he had finished the sermon, advised and incited, it was thought, by that same Alonso Pérez, he delivered a very daring, bitter, excessive and unbridled speech against the worthy Grand Master, who certainly did not deserve that his ears should hear such daring and vituperative words as that friar spoke against him that day, accusing him of so many and such horrible crimes and wrong doings that it would really be very tedious to have to particularize them here, scandalizing all the hearers against him in an astounding fashion and exhorting them to his destruction.

In fact, that friar went so far in his rantings that the King, not being able to stand his discordant mouthings, signaled him with the cane he had within his curtains, ordering him to be quiet. This he did very quickly, and left the church. It may be true that the friar did not name or expressly say: "The Grand Master of Santiago, don Álvaro de Luna, does this or that," but he spoke in a general way:

"A person, a person whom you all know and is in the church right now, etc..."

The worthy Grand Master, as one who did not put up with such discord, immediately approached the Bishop of Burgos and said to him:

"Reverend Bishop, bear in mind that it is your duty to find out from that friar why he let himself say so many empty insults and dissolute follies on such a day and time, and who put him up to it. For it certainly is not to be believed that such daring came from him, without the inducement of someone else."

The Bishop replied: "Leave this to me, sir, for I shall have him apprehended at once."

He set to work on it and the friar was arrested and put in the episcopal prison.

After the service for the day was concluded, the King went to his palace and the Grand Master accompanied him. Because it was already late, for it was past noon, he took leave of the King, considerably annoyed by what the friar had so presumptuously and outrageously vociferated, for his heart at once told him that this had proceeded from his evil servant, the traitor Alonso Pérez, with the aim of irritating and arousing the people against him. It certainly seems, oh wicked Alonso Pérez, that although you are from Vivero, a name which means and is thought to be derived from "vivir," *to live,* you knowingly wish to destroy your life, and that in these deeds you embraced death with both arms and all your will, and you embraced the traitor Judas, whose true follower you showed yourself to be; for on such days and in such a week did he plan the death of his Lord, just as you planned that of your lord. But consider that the punishment is prepared for you and is very near in this world, to say nothing of that which you will receive endlessly in the next. For your deeds are what are to follow you, and they will follow you!

The loyal Grand Master, after he had returned home and eaten, went up to the tower, the key to which he kept, as has been written, and from there he had Fernando de Ribadeneyra summoned. When he had come, he asked him what he had thought of the raving of that friar. Fernando replied, saying: "To be sure, sir, it seemed very bad to me, and the worst I see is that your lordship knows very well how things are going and you refuse to remedy them. You see that this wretched traitor, Alonso Pérez, is plotting and agitating these things against you, and you will see worse, if you do not move against him soon, and let him go and do not let me kill him, for I really do not doubt that God would be served by the death of such a traitor, to avoid the very serious and great evils that he is scheming, and in the eyes of God and the world it would be looked upon as a good and virtuous deed and loyal duty."

The worthy Grand Master replied: "Certainly, until now I would have prefered that this man would somehow desist and leave that wickedness in which he has been moving, but since we cannot dissuade him from it, let his evil be upon his head and his death be upon his guilt. Therefore send him to me, for I have prepared an artifice by which he will be paid the wages he deserves."

Fernando de Ribadeneyra replied: "Well, sir, do not put it off any longer; if you do, it will be worse for your estate and honor, to say nothing of your personal safety; for I have learned with certainty that the King has sent for don Alvaro, the son of the Count of Plazencia, not much of a friend to you, to come with his people whenever he is ordered."

While the good Grand Master and Fernando de Ribadeneyra were talking, the Bishop of Burgos and the Relator came to his lodging to talk with him; and before they came, the Grand Master had already sent someone to summon that wicked Alonso Pérez. In the discussion that the Bishop and the Relator had with the Grand Master, the Bishop said to him: "Sir, I have come to tell your lordship what has taken place with that mad and senseless friar. I have not been able to get anything from him, except that he says he was inspired to say what he did by a revelation from God, and that never was he persuaded to it by anyone in the world."

Then the Grand Master said to the Bishop: "Reverend Father, have him questioned as his habit and the laws require, for it is a mockery to say that a fat, red, worldly friar had a revelation from God."

The Bishop said that he would do so. But our history, making no further mention of the affair of that friar, goes on to tell how the Bishop and the Relator left the Grand Master, and there remained in his presence, up in the tower where he was, the iniquitous Alonso Pérez and Fernando de Ribadeneyra. In the meantime, the Grand Master had summoned Juan de Luna, who came to the tower without delay, and there the Grand Master withdrew with him for a secret talk in a room that was in the highest part of the tower. He told him in a few words that it was his will, after careful deliberation, that he and Fernando de Ribadeneyra should cast the traitor Alonso Pérez off that tower, as he had already spoken and agreed on with that same Ribadeneyra, and that he himself did not wish to lay his hands on such a villainous figure of a man as that.

Juan de Luna answered the Grand Master, saying he kissed his hand for the great favor he did him, and the great trust he showed in him. The Grand Master replied, withouth making a long speech, but telling him how he always considered him like his own son. Then he told him to go to Alonso Pérez and to send in Fernando de Ribadeneyra. When the latter came, the Grand Master said: "I have just spoken with Juan de Luna, and he says he is pleased and happy to help you throw this wicked man down there" —for the Grand Master had already pointed out to Fernando the place from which they were to throw him, and showed it later to Juan de Luna— "therefore do it in such a manner that the railing will give way and fall with him, so that those who see it below will think and say that the railing fell with him as he leaned against it. But I certainly think my heart would be pained if, before he died,

I did not make him openly see his wickedness, through his own handwriting, for I have here the King's letters, and his, as to how they are seeking to destroy me."

Then Fernando de Ribadeneyra said to the Grand Master: "Sir, I think that would be very good."

"Then call him here to me," said the Grand Master.

So all three entered the room where the Grand Master was. He directed his words to his disloyal servant, saying to him: "Tell me, Alonso Pérez, do you recognize this handwriting?"

Looking at it, Alonso Pérez said, "Yes, sir."

The Grand Master said, "Well, whose is it?"

Alonso Pérez said, "It is the King's."

"And this other one," said the Grand Master, "whose is it?"

Alonso Pérez said, "Sir, it is mine."

Then the Grand Master said to Fernando, "Read those letters." And Fernando read them to Alonso Pérez. The latter, after they were read, was very alarmed, to the point of death, and with good reason, for it was nearby. The good Grand Master spoke at once, saying to him: "Certainly, since you have refused to be dissuaded from the wickedness that you have plotted and prepared against me, by all the reasons and admonitions I have given you, it is fitting that that oath which I had you swear to before Fernando, who is here present, be carried out."

After the Grand Master had spoken, he ordered Juan de Luna and Fernando de Ribadeneyra to take that wicked, perverse and treacherous servant of his and throw him off the tower railing. They set to work without delay. Thus did the traitorous servant end his days, on Good Friday, after sunset. And in him was fulfilled that proverb which says: "He who lives evilly will die evilly."

Concerning what happened after the death of Alonso Pérez

In all the things the illustrious Grand Master did, his principal endeavor was that the King, his lord, would not be angered at him for any thing, and that neither his Majesty nor anyone else could accuse him of ever having angered his royal Majesty. It was for this reason, as our history has already told, that he arranged to have the traitor who was seeking his death and destruction killed, so that his death could be attributed to a chance event and not to a planned and deliberate act. To sustain and carry out this illusion, even though it is a vexatious and serious thing to make people believe that the true is false and the false true, at the moment that Alonso Pérez fell, so that people would think he had fallen through a wretched and unfortunate mishap, Juan de Luna and Fernando de Ribadeneyra immediately rushed down the tower stairway, shouting, "Down, down to the street, for Alonso Pérez has fallen off the tower in an unfortunate accident."

At the time they were going down shouting like that, Gonzalo Chacón, the steward of the Grand Master and Knight Commander of Montiel, of whom we have spoken before, [1] was at the door to the stairway which went up to the tower. When he saw them coming down with such a noise, thinking it was some evil that had been committed against the Grand Master, his lord, he grasped a dagger that he wore at his waist and told them, "You go down if you wish, for my lord, the Grand Master, told me to stay here."

Those two knights and many other people who were in the Grand Master's house at that time went down to see what it was all about, and so many went to look that no one was left in the house except Gonzalo Chacón. They discovered that Alonso Pérez de Vivero was dead, for he had hit his head on a corner of a stone bridge that was next to the Grand Master's house and his brains had spattered on the walls.

In the meantime, while things were in that state of confusion, Gonzalo Chacón went quickly up to where his lord, the Grand Master, was. The latter said to him. "Chacón, did you ever see such a miracle and misfortune as befell Alonso Pérez, for a railing fell down with him while he was leaning against it. Go quickly, for heaven's sake, and have him taken to one of those houses, in case he can be healed."

Gonzalo Chacón immediately went where his master ordered him, and descended the stairs. As he saw that the house was empty, he thought it would be a lack of precaution to leave his master alone at such a time, for it might be that, given the great and violent hubbub that was going on, some servant of Alonso Pérez de Vivero's, seeing his master like that before his eyes, might come

---

[1] Gonzalo Chacón was also probably the author of this chronicle.

in a fit of rage to kill the Grand Master himself, finding him alone and thinking that he had had him flung down. Certainly, a sensible and wise thought for a young knight! So Gonzalo Chacón stopped at once at the foot of the stairs, and at that moment, Juan de Luna, Fernando de Ribadeneyra and many other people with them came back and told the Grand Master how Alonso Pérez had hit the corner of the bridge and had died immediately.

At this, the Grand Master made a show of great sorrow before all the people and, putting on the appearance of a person almost beside himself, entered his room. Then he sent for a servant of Alonso Pérez', whom this same Alonso Pérez had greatly trusted. This person was present in the street when his master fell, and when he saw that he was dead, he removed from his finger a signet ring that he wore and withdrew quite sorrowfully, to wherever he went, so that he could not be found when the Grand Master sent for him. Then he ordered them to call Garci Sánchez de Valladolid, who was the paymaster for Alonso Pérez. When he had come before him, the Grand Master began to weep grievously, afflicting himself in an amazing fashion and putting on a semblance of great sadness, saying he had lost the best servant he ever had or hoped to have, and saying that, although Alonso Pérez was dead, he was the one left with the dolorous, just and heavy pain and hardship of his death, and saying also that he had lost that day the pillar and support of his deeds, his household and his estates. The discreet Grand Master fashioned other expressions of painful sentiment, saying: "See, gentlemen, what repose was reserved for me in the age I am at, for on this single servant rested all my deeds; all my affairs depended on him, and I along with them."

He uttered many similar expressions of sorrow and regret, mixed with not a few tears and sighs. Finally, ceasing his lament and almost coming to himself, he said: "However, friend Garci Sánchez, since it cannot be helped, let us give thanks to God for everything that is done; and be certain that I shall look after Juan de Vivero, Alonso Pérez' son, and his other children and servants as I would my own. And so that you may see that my words conform with my deeds, I have already sent to beg the King's favor, that he grant the post of chief treasurer to Juan de Vivero. Therefore, go tell him so at once and console him and yourself and all the other servants of his father; and may God send his consolation everywhere, for it is sorely needed."

It certainly cannot be denied that in this affair the eminent Grand Master made manifest his great wisdom and understanding, for as the wise man says: "Worthy of being a lord is that person who, along with the other virtue, honor and valor he may have, knows sometimes, when the situation demands it, how to show pleasure, even though he may not have it, or sadness, even though he may not feel it, for such do the nature and fickleness of the world require." It is certain that Pompey was the capital enemy of that Gaius Julius Caesar, of whom the historians tell so many praises, and also, Julius Caesar pursued Pompey with bitter, implacable hatred; but when they showed him his head after he had been killed, Roman history tells how he shed tears at his death. For as the worthy doctrine of St. Paul teaches people, it is wisdom to rejoice with the joyful and to weep with the sorrowful.

But getting back to our account, Garci Sánchez went off and found Juan de Vivero and the servants of his father, Alonso Pérez, lamenting greatly and tearing their hair, and he accompanied them in their weeping. After he had mourned with them for some time, he found a way to get them to listen to what he wanted to say, and, silence having been established, he repeated the words that the Grand Master had said, with which Juan de Vivero was somewhat comforted, since nothing else could be done.

Then he and the servants of Alonso Pérez went straightway to the Grand Master and found him in his chamber. Juan de Vivero entered, weeping and tearing his hair and making a great lament; the Grand Master, too, renewed his weeping with him. After that, he began to say many comforting words to him, telling him, among other things, "that if he had lost a father, he had gained a father, for he was taking him under his care like a son, out of respect for his father and the many services he had done him. Therefore he should join his household and consider it as his father had done; for beyond what Juan de Vivero held from the Grand Master in emoluments, he would give him more and would do him many favors. And he should be comforted, for the King had already granted the chief treasurership for him, as his father had held it."

Both Juan de Vivero and Garci Sánchez kissed the Grand Master's hands for this, saying many words of exceedingly great gratitude, and similarly making him many affectionate offers, Juan de Vivero saying that, if his father had served his lordship well, no less would he do with all his strength, and that they would resemble each other in deeds. When these acts and words were over, they took leave of the Grand Master, for it was very late at night now, and went to their dwellings. But before they left, the Grand Master commanded Garci Sánchez to have the body of Alonso Pérez taken at once to be buried in Valladolid, in the Monastery of St. Benedict of that city, previously mentioned, where he himself proposed to be interred.

At the time Alonso Pérez was killed, the King was in the Cathedral, at evening services, and when he was told the news of his death, he was indeed much grieved by it and showed no small alteration in his expression. It was thought that this great alteration was probably caused because the King thought that Alonso Pérez, before he died, might have revealed at length the dealings and affairs he was involved in...

> (Gonzalo Chacón, *Crónica de don Álvaro de Luna,* chapters 113, 114 and 115.)

THE DEATH OF DON ÁLVARO DE LUNA

After thirty-five years in power, and three months after the death of Alonso Pérez, the great Constable of Castile, don Álvaro de Luna, was brought low. The chapter that relates his execution in Valladolid is one of the most moving passages in fifteenth century Spanish literature. The fact that Chacón was deeply prejudiced in favor of Luna and overlooked his faults does not take away a whit from its emotive value. There are decidedly rhetorical devices employed —the use of the historical present, the direct appeal to the reader, the apostrophe to God— but the overwhelming impression is the personal emotion of the author in the face of this tragedy, which took place on June 2, 1453.

On the death of the best knight and greatest uncrowned
lord who lived in all the Spains at that time, the good
Grand Master of Santiago.

(In an introductory paragraph, the author explains, with
religious reasoning, why he calls don Álvaro "fortunate".)

Then Diego López de Estúñiga set out from the encampment
near Escalona for the town of Portillo, where the fortunate Grand
Master was imprisoned, and he carried with him, as is already
written, the sentence of death that had been handed down against
him and the writ for its execution, and he also brought a writ for
the warden of the fortress of Portillo, to hand over the Grand Master to him. Diego López came straight to Valladolid, gathered there
the people he thought to be necessary to bring the Grand Master
under good guard, and proceeded to Portillo. But first he arranged
at the Monastery of St. Francis in Valladolid that a very famous
sage and master of theology who was there at the time, named
Master Alfonso Espina, should set out the following day on the
road to Portillo and that at the passage of the River Duero he
should feign a chance meeting with the Grand Master, who knew
him well, and thence should return with him to Valladolid. Talking
about one thing and another, he was to withdraw with the Grand
Master, saying he wanted to tell him something in secret, and there
he was to reveal to him that he was being taken to be killed, for
those who had gone for him told him nothing (as they had arranged
among themselves) except that the King ordered him to go to Valladolid.

When all this was put into effect, the monk withdrew from the
others to talk with the fortunate Grand Master; and beginning
his talk with some remarks by way of a harangue, which he certainly
knew how to do well, for he was a great preacher, he finally notified
him in the best and most comforting words he could, that they were
taking him to be executed, exhorting him, as a Catholic and faithful
Christian, to take strength from the true and holy faith of Jesus
Christ and to confess and repent his sins with the greatest contrition
possible. The fortunate Grand Master, after he heard what the venerable monk told him, thanked him warmly for it, gave a great sigh
raising his eyes to heaven, and said only: "Blessed art thou, oh
Lord, who rule and govern the world."

He then very fondly entreated the monk not to leave him until the hour of his death. The honest monk assured him on this score and he was very content and consoled thereby. And right there on the road, as they went along, the good Grand Master scrutinized his conscience and began to confess his sins to Master Alfonso Espina. Throughout the journey, which must have been almost two leagues long, and they travelled very slowly, the fortunate Grand Master continued his confession, showing great contrition for his errors. Then, when they were almost at the entrance to the town, leaving off his confession for the moment, and still accompanied by that venerable monk and a companion of the latter, he was taken by Diego López de Estúñiga to be lodged in some houses that belonged to a gentleman named Alonso de Estúñiga, which are on the street called the Street of the French, where this same fortunate Grand Master was wont to stay in times past, and Diego López himself asked the monks not to leave him, but accompany him that night. This they willingly acceded to, and did.

To be sure, all three had little sleep that night, for the fortunate Grand Master was still ordering his soul and unburdening his conscience and, also, arranging his will and the distribution of his wealth among those places and people to whom he understood himself to be obligated. Thus did he and the monks pass almost the entire night.

When it was daylight, the fortunate Grand Master heard mass in his room and, as he was advised that his life was to end in a short while, asked to be brought a few cherries and a little bread, but he ate very little of either.

In the main square of Valladolid, near the previously mentioned Monastery of St. Francis, there was erected a new scaffold for this new thing, the like of which was never seen in Castile, that a great lord should die, sentenced to death by the King and with the charge publicly proclaimed by the town crier. After the scaffold was set up and furbished as befitted such a deed, with a rich carpet spread on the flooring, Diego López de Estúñiga, accompanied by armed men, went to his lodging to get the fortunate Grand Master, who at that moment was talking with his confessor. They told him to come down from his room and ride on his mule, which was saddled and prepared; so he came down without delay, stil accompanied by the monks.

The trumpet sounds with dolorous, sad and discordant note. The crier begins his lying proclamation. Our history calls it lying because it was undoubtedly so. For consider, you who are reading, what a deed was that, and what a baseless, unfounded proclamation. For notwithstanding the fact that all who were in the King's council at that time —with the exception, as we have stated, of the Archbishop of Toledo— took part in handing down the sentence that the Grand Master should die (and the Relator Fernando Díez de Toledo, who to be sure was a man of sharp and cunning talent, was with them), and they all attended to drawing up the proclamation that was to be read when the fortunate Grand Master was being taken to be killed, yet they could find nothing on which to base and compose that proclamation, or give it any reason or pretext, except to say "that he had seized the person of the King." Oh Lord, what a false, and obviously false, proclamation that was! For if he had seized the King, the King would not have had the power to bring him to his death.

So the good and fortunate Grand Master rode on his mule, with the same expression and appearance of tranquility with which he used to ride in past times of cheerful and smiling fortune. The mule, covered with mourning, and he, in a long black cape. And just as it is told that the martyrs went with joyful countenance to receive death and martyrdom for the faith of Jesus Christ, so did the fortunate Grand Master go, with no perturbation showing on his face, to drain the draught of death, knowing within himself that he was innocent and guiltless toward the King, his lord, and that they were inflicting on him the death he was about to receive because he had always acted with goodness, virtue and loyalty toward him. He strengthened himself in God, believing that He loved him well in that occurrence and wanted him for Himself, and that it pleased Him that he should receive that publicly proclaimed death by steel for his other sins. For it is not to be doubted that they are fortunate who die in the holy Catholic faith, and die as Catholic Christians, and the cause of their death is that they acted virtuously and suffer for it. Witness: that true God and Man Himself, who says in His Gospel: "Blessed are they who suffer persecution for justice, for theirs is the kingdom of Heaven"...

So the fortunate Grand Master went on his mule, as we have described, still accompanied by that reverend clergyman, and was brought to the scaffold. When he reached it, he dismounted from the mule and unconcernedly ascended the steps of the scaffold; when he arrived at the top and found himself on the platform where the rug was laid, he removed the hat he was wearing and threw it to one of his pages, whose name we have already told was Morales. The fortunate Grand Master himself arranged the folds of the clothing he was wearing and, because the executioner told him it would be necessary to tie his hands, or at least his thumbs, so that he would not create any anxiety or try to hold off the knife in fear of death, he took out the thong from a pouch he was wearing, one of those in use at the time, which were almost like little game bags, and gave it to the headsman, who tied his thumbs with it.

And then, as he entrusted his soul to God, the executioner separated his head from his shoulders. See in this occurrence, oh reader, a thing that certainly should be worthy of notice and even of being considered miraculous; for notwithstanding the fact that when they were taking the fortunate Grand Master to be put to death —one cannot say that they were taking him to execute justice on him, for they killed him against all justice—, the people who gathered to witness it, all acted as they ordinarily do on such occasions, not with sad gestures and faces, but like people who are going to see something that does not happen every day, and especially going to see such an act, never before witnessed in Castile. Yet, at the moment the executioner took the knife in his hands, all the people together, men and women, those present in the square as well as those standing in the windows of the houses near the square, fell first into a deep silence, as if they all, consciously and under heavy penalty, had been ordered to keep quiet.

Right after this, at the moment that the executioner was putting the sharp and whetted knife to the throat of the fortunate Grand Master, there arose from among all such a dolorous and heart-felt lament, such a loud and tearful outcry and a clamor of such sorrow and grief, as if each person there, male and female, had seen his father or some other dearly beloved person killed. So dies the glorious, the famous, the virtuous and fortunate Grand Master and Constable of Castile, in the manner the history has described. God rest his soul; as one certainly ought piously to believe, that he is in the company of His chosen ones; and so was it revealed not many days afterward to a man of saintly life, that he was in a good place.

He was ordered killed by his beloved and obeyed lord, the King, who in ordering his death, can truthfully be said to have killed himself, for after his death he lived only a year and fifty days, all of which, it must be stated, were days of sorrow and hardship. For he was very often repentant of his deed, and his servants would find him weeping bitterly for the death of his loyal Grand Master. Too, he fell ill shortly after with a serious attack of quartan fever which lasted many months, so that with it, and the after-effects, he never enjoyed a healthy day after that. And there were some who said that it was only the gnawing worm of his conscience that killed him, reminding him constantly of the great cruelty he had used against his most loyal of loyal subjects.

(Gonzalo Chacón, *Crónica de don Alvaro de Luna*, chapter 128.)

WARFARE

The Capture of a Moorish City

Warfare, of course, assumes comsiderable importance in writings of our period. The traditional enemies were the Moors; the official attitude was, as it had been for centuries, that they were interlopers on Christian soil, and the ultimate goal was to drive them from the Peninsula. In truth, however, the people in the Christian kingdoms, and especially Castile, the leader, were so busily engaged in internal squabbles and struggles for power that no concerted or sustained action against the Kingdom of Granada was possible. The "Moorish question" was dealt with as often through diplomacy as through force of arms, by playing off one faction in Granada against another, by agreeing to truces or by accepting Moorish rulers as vassals. The most important military action was carried out during the minority of the King, when Prince Fernando, the regent, captured Antequera. A few campaigns were waged, as in 1431, when Castilian troops penetrated as far as the plain of Granada and burned towns and fields, but nothing permanent was accomplished. In 1434, Rodrigo Manrique, the Knight Commander of Segura, captured the stronghold of Huescar. It was an isolated victory, rather than part of a coherent campaign. The description of the event is from Manrique's letter to the King, informing him of the town's capture. It offers an interesting account of the type of military activity carried out in the border areas to the south.

The letter is taken from the so-called *Crónica del halconero de Juan II* (*Chronicle of the Falconer of Juan II*). This history, incomplete today, was written by Pedro Carrillo de Huete, of whom little is know except that he maintained a strict neutrality in the power struggles of the period. His chronicle's claim to importance is that in it are utilized some two hundred actual documents, which makes it an extremely valuable source for history.

Rodrigo Manrique, the youthful hero of the capture of Huescar and writer of the letter, was later one of the grandees most opposed to don Alvaro de Luna. He lived a long life: in 1474 he was elected Grand Master of the Order of Santiago and in 1476 he took part in the battle of Toro on behalf of the Catholic Monarchs. He died the same year and was immortalized by his son, Jorge Manrique, in the famous *Coplas por la muerte de su padre*. The *Coplas* were translated to English in the nineteenth century by Longfellow.

The letter that Rodrigo Manrique sent to the King, concerning the capture of Huescar.

"Most excellent and virtuous lord: May it please your Grace to know that, while I was in the town of Siles, thinking of how I might do something that would be of service to you, especially concerning the capture of this city of Huescar, there came to me Lope de Vergara, squire to my brother Diego Manrique, with a letter from Juan Enríquez, your servant and my cousin, in which he informed me that his desire was to serve your Grace as always, and that he had been told by certain leaders, especially Ruy Díaz (whom your Grace converted to Christianity), Gonzalo García and Sancho Gómez, the leaders of Quesada, how they thought this town could be scaled, but that very vigorous men were needed to attack it, since they knew that there were many good people within to defend it, as will indeed be seen later on, my lord.

In short, sire, after I had received this letter (and our Lord knows how happy I was with it), notwithstanding the dealings I had been engaged in before on this very subject, recognizing the great service that would accrue to your Grace even though some danger might befall me, I set to work on it at once. And I sent Lope de Vergara back to Juan Enríquez, requesting him to come to me.

He did so, but on the way he had to go with my uncle, Fernando Alvarez, to put Alicun to the test. When I saw that he was not coming, I was quite angry; but I thought it might be well to make a raid against this town, to make them think I would not come again so soon, so they would feel more secure, and also to look over the town, although I had seen it other times. Of what was done at that time, your Grace has already been informed.

When I returned from this foray, sire, I immediately spoke with Juan Enríquez, whom I had left when I set out on the raid, for he arrived the very day I departed. We agreed that certain squires of his and mine would go back to probe where the scaling ladder might best be set up. They started out at once with Ruy Díaz, who was to show them where it was to be done. They arrived and spent two hours right up against the walls, and saw conditions in quite a different state than we were to find them when I came. They came back to me, but did not find me, for I had set out for the town of Ubeda in search of men. I spoke with them when I returned, and they told me they thought it could be done, inasmuch as there were only four watchmen and a man who made the round. Your Grace may well believe that I was very pleased at this news, thinking I would find it like that. I then sent for Manuel de Benavides at your court, and wrote to Garci Méndez, who sent me his son, Gómez de Sotomayor, with twenty-five horsemen and twenty foot-soldiers. He and his men were well prepared for everything concerning the undertaking.

The Commander of Beas also came, sire, with fourteen horsemen and as many as a hundred foot-soldiers; the Governor of Yeste with twenty horsemen and twenty foot-soldiers; from Alcaraz came Gonzalo Díaz de Bustamante with ten horsemen and thirty foot-soldiers, and Juan de Claramonte came with him; and from Ubeda came Diego de la Cueva with eight horsemen, and Diego López de San Martín (whom your Grace exiled to Hornos), and Rodrigo de Pareja with four horsemen, and Pedro Sánchez de la Calancha with fourteen horsemen; and from Campo de Montiel ten horsemen and ten foot-soldiers came to me. In short, sire, all together there must have been two hundred horsemen and six hundred foot-soldiers.

Now, sire, when these people had gathered, I set forth on Wednesday, the third day of this month, and reached the town on Friday, just about midnight. I dismounted a half league away, and Juan Enríquez asked me for seventy warriors and two hundred foot-soldiers to go with the scaling ladders, and he arranged the men as he understood was necessary for the deed. I, sire, left all the other mounted troops with Gómez de Sotomayor, the Commander of Beas and Alvaro de Madrid, and taking Manuel de Benavides and Pedro de Prado with me, accompanied Juan Enríquez to have the men scale the wall.

We arrived in rank at the moat, which is very deep. When we came, we found that the night guards had been changed and were keeping as sharp a vigil as ever I saw, with two patrols that crossed the very place that the ladders were to be set up. The result was, sire, that it was very doubtful that the deed could be carried through; but taking strength in our Lord and in your royal Grace's very good fortune, the venture was begun in this manner:

Juan Enríquez set up his ladder as Ruy Díaz showed us the entrance of the moat. The ladder was set up while the patrols were passing; they were talking in their Arabic, saying that if God delivered them that night they would have no fear, for I do believe, sire, that they had some suspicion of our presence. The ladder was put in place right after a patrol passed, and Lope de Frías and Pedro de Curiel, squires of Juan Enríque's, went up at once to hold the ladders, as they usually do. Then, sire, your vassal Alvar Rodríguez de Córdoba, the *alcaide* of Segura, went up, armed, followed by Pero Sánchez de Fornos, also your Grace's vassal, and Pedro de Beas.

And before the *alcaide* could get all the way up, the night guard heard him and threw down a pannier of stones on him. Nevertheless, he continued climbing. At the shouts of the watchman, the defense walls and roofs were seized by the Moors, and your Grace should know that quite a few of my squires who went up the ladder were wounded or killed by two Moors who held a loop-hole in the tower.

They would have done even greater damage, if it had not been for the *alcaide,* who killed one of them, and the other jumped to a roof. But, sire, killed there on the wall were the Ceciliano, the brother of the *alcaide,* Pedro Sánchez de Fornos, Juan de León, García de Albuera, and my squires Nicolas and Furtuno; and Juan de Ribera, Pero Alvarez de la Torre, Juan de Quirós, Lope de Vergara, Fernando de Molina, Juan de Treviño and Rodrigo de Mendoza were wounded. They were in such shape, sire, that the least wounded could hardly go forward.

Then my standard bearer went up, for the trumpeter had been the sixth to ascend and was already, with great courage, blowing so boldly that he inspired great fear in the Moors. My uncle, Manuel de Benavides, mounted after the standard bearer; and the *alcaide* of Yeste, who was up and had fought very well, followed him, in spite of being seriously wounded, as did the others who were able. He went along the wall, fighting and winning towers, until he found the way down to the gate. He descended and found himself in considerable difficulty breaking it, but finally got it opened.

I entered through the gate with the rest of the men, and we went on fighting through the streets until we drove the enemy into the fortress and into certain towers that they held on the defense wall. In this struggle a great number of people, both ours and the enemy's, were wounded. And the truth is that some twelve or fifteen Moors were killed there. I assure your Grace that all that day, Saturday, and all that night, the fighting never ceased, as we went capturing their houses and mining them, and throwing up barricades across the streets; all of which they opposed vigorously.

The next day, Sunday, the *Cabçani* [1] arrived with all the men of Baza and its valley, who must have numbered some five hundred horsemen and not many foot-soldiers. They came as far as the gardens that day, so close to the town that they could talk with the people in the fortress. Sire, I did not have enough men to resist them in the field, for I had quite enough to do in the city. The Moors, realizing how few men we were, put down a ladder from one of the towers they held on the wall, and a considerable number of their crossbowmen began to ascend. Others came and opened the gate they held adjoining the fortress, so the knights who had arrived at the gate could enter.

When I saw what the situation was and the great trouble that could come to us from that direction, I took some ten men at arms with me and went out to do them battle. And it pleased our Lord, and that good courage which your Grace inspires in our hearts from where you are, that I captured that gate by force and closed them up by the gates of the fortress. Of the forty or fifty who were there, some seven or eight were left dead. When the knights saw that, they swerved off a little. I, sire, was wounded there by an arrow from a crossbow that pierced my brassard and my right arm.

---

[1] The *cabçani* is a Moorish leader.

Elsewhere, sire, I sent Alvaro de Madrid with some men at arms, and he went capturing and sapping from house to house, fighting always with the enemy, until he chased them into another tower that they held on the wall. Because of the large force that was attacking, I sent Manuel de Benavides to him, and I could not begin to describe to your Grace the hardships that he and Alvaro suffered there. For, my lord, the smoke that was sent up to impede the mines was alone enough to kill a thousand men, to say nothing of the fierce combat that they also gave them.

In short, sire, such was our work all that Sunday. Meanwhile, no help came, which we desperately needed, considering the shape the men were in, both from wounds and from fatigue. Indeed, sire, your Captain General Fernán Alvarez, seeing the great service that could accrue to your Grace, would have come at once to succor me, if it had not been for the confusion there was in certain signals I had arranged. On Thursday night, before the venture was undertaken, he had been given a letter from me, by which I informed him of the deed to which I was going, and, although I was not certain of finishing it, I asked him to send some men to Quesada, to succor me sometime Saturday if the deed could be accomplished and my messenger should arrive.

I advised your *Adelantado* of Cazorla in the same manner, except that the warning letter was given him on Friday night; in it, sire, was contained the venture to which I was going, and word that he would receive a messenger of mine sometime Saturday, if there were any need. I wrote the same way to García de Cárdenas.

As I entered the city of Huescar, I immediately sent off my messengers. Because I could not write, nor was it reasonable to leave off fighting to write, I sent a ring of mine to the *adelantado* and a hood to García de Cárdenas, as a sign of credence, so they would come; and I sent word to the *adelantado* to send his men from Cazorla to Quesada, not knowing whether Fernán Alvarez' people, whom I had requested, would have come there. But, sire, as one who does not neglect the things he understands to be to your service, he had already sent his nephew and my cousin, Pedro de Quiñones, there.

When the latter received the message, he immediately rode with sixty men at arms and a hundred foot-soldiers, and never stopped until he got to me, at midnight on Sunday, with a great supply of water. At that time, sire, the Moors had their encampment in the gardens of the city, and he got through with considerable danger to himself and his men. Both in his coming, which we certainly needed, and while he was there, he did much for your Grace's service, taking charge of one of the mines and of certain towers on the wall; while fighting in them some of his squires were wounded, but he deported himself well and like a knight.

Monday next, at dawn, the *adelantado* of Cazorla arrived with one hundred horsemen and a few foot-soldiers that he snatched up to come right away. Without a doubt, sire, he underwent much hardship in travelling all that night, for the road was bad. As soon as he arrived, I went out to meet him and told him certain things: first, that he should not enter the city, since I thought he had people who could be out in the field; and second, that with the men he had and others I would give him who were with me, he should recapture our water, which the Moors had taken from us, although, sire, there are wells in the city. I also told him to make a showing before the Moors, so they would realize the help I had received and would not press me so hard as they had the day before.

As one desirous of your service, sire, he set to the task, carrying out all these things, and remained outside, very near the Moors, all day long. Finally he had to come into the city, and at once the Moorish cavalry rushed forward, along with many foot-soldiers. The foot-soldiers pressed forward to mount the ladder they had set up, and some of them got up with as many provisions as they could. But in their ascent a number were killed, and some of our crossbowmen were wounded.

Tuesday morning, the Moorish horsemen and foot-soldiers took positions in the garden, near the city, as they usually did. It was agreed by the *adelantado* and us that it would be well for him to go outside, since another hundred horsemen of his had arrived that night, and that only the soldiers necessary for the mines would remain with Pedro de Quiñones and myself. All the other mounted men, both mine and his, would go out with him. I asked my cousin, Juan Enríquez, even though he had an arrow wound in his right arm, and the Commander of Beas to go out into the field, and also the *alcaide* of Segura, although he was wounded. My cousin set to the task, paying little attention to his wound, such was his desire to serve your Grace.

The *adelantado* sallied forth, with many other knights, and placed himself very near the Moorish knights and their foot-soldiers, skirmishing with them; many horses and men were wounded and killed on both sides. So they stayed, from morning until evening. In the evening, news arrived that Fernán Alvarez was coming, and I sent word of this to the *adelantado*. He kept on approaching the Moors and fighting with them and, in my opinion, there were twice as many Moorish horsemen as he had, and their foot-soldiers were four times as many as his.

But God help me, sire, he attacked them like the man he was, and routed them. As for how the pursuit was pressed and how many died, I do believe that he is writing this to your Grace, for he could see it better than I, who was inside, guarding and defending the town. But at this moment I saw the banners of Fernán Alvarez coming into view, and I went forth to meet him and asked him if he wanted to enter the town to rest, or what he wanted to do. He answered that he was coming to defend the field and that he proposed to set up out there, for he trusted that the person who had taken the town could defend it.

So he did, and set up his camp outside the city. As the Moors saw that the field could be controlled by Fernán Alvarez and the others who were there, they came the next day, Wednesday, to parley and offered their conditions. None was received that day; Fernán Alvarez, the *adelantado,* myself and the gentlemen here regretted not having gone out to the parley, seeing the great disservice that could accrue to your Grace from not having done so, in view of the supplies and great number of people that were in the fortress.

But they came back to talk the next day. In conclusion, since these gentlemen saw that their departure from the castle, however it might be accomplished, had to be attained, we guaranteed their lives, that they could leave in freedom, taking nothing, neither arms nor any other chattels, and each man could wear only one outfit of clothing and each woman, two. They all departed this Thursday morning and we took possession of the fortress.

Sire, I did not wish to write your Grace until the castle was captured, so that the person who went might bring your Grace the complete news. Concerning all these things, which I could not write your Grace as fully as they happened, I am sending you my servant Alfonso de Córdoba. I beg your Highness to show him favor, first for what he did in your service, and then for the news that it has pleased God I might send you through him, and to give him faith and credence in all those things he will tell your royal Grace on my behalf.

Also, sire, may it please you to have sent here at once such provisions as your Grace may see fit, both of men at arms and foot-soldiers as well as all the other things of which the bearer will inform you. For the present, what I ask is that your Grace will grant me that fifth part of the booty that belongs to you; for, sire, I will indeed have need of it, just for the wounds, the dead beasts and other wants. This your Grace may believe.

May it please our Lord to guard and increase your royal estate, and grant me grace to serve your Highness with similar services. From your town of Huescar, the twelfth of the present month, your humble servant who kisses your hands and feet.

Rodrigo Manrique."

This Rodrigo Manrique was twenty-two years old when he accomplished this honorable feat.

(Pedro Carrillo de Huete, *Crónica del halconero de Juan II,* chapter 169.)

Because of the unstable political conditions within Castile, the Christians were unable to pursue the Reconquest, and the Moors, although they had their own internal dissensions and revolts, sometimes were able to take advantage of the situation to recapture lands that had been lost earlier. They never posed a really serious threat to Christian dominance, but it was a distressing situation for the Christian kingdoms. The town of Huescar, which Rodrigo Manrique won from the Moors in 1434, was lost to them again in 1447.

How the Moors of the Kingdom of Granada heard of
the discord in the Kingdom of Castile, and entered the
Christian lands and seized certain towns and fortresses.

When the Moors of Granada heard of the upheavals and discord that were taking place in this kingdom of Castile at this time, in view of which they could not be opposed, they resolved to invade the Christians' lands. And they removed great booty, both men and women as well as much livestock, on several occasions.

The worst was that they took by force certain towns and fortresses which the Christians had won at great expense and hardship, with deaths and spilling of Christian blood. Those who in their own selfish and malicious interest have been and are the cause of the seditions and discord of this realm are responsible for this. Especially, at different times this year, the Moors captured the following towns and fortresses: the town and fortress of Arenas, the town and fortress of Benamaurel, the town and fortress of Huescar, and the town and fortress of Velez el Blanco. These towns and fortresses were a great guard and defense for Christian territory, and also a fine gateway by which to enter the Moorish lands and win further territory and safely take out much booty. They were lost because they were not provisioned, and it was not the fault of their *alcaides,* for they often asked the King to order them supplied and provisioned, but the King could not do it because of the great need he was in at the time, due to the aforementioned seditions and discord. Woe be to those who have caused this!

(Pedro Carrillo de Huete, *Crónica del halconero de Juan II,* chapter 354.)

The Battle of Olmedo

Warfare was directed more often against other Christians than against the Moors. The impression one gets of most of the reign of Juan II is that there was an endless chain of rebellions and disturbances, almost all aimed at destroying the power of the favorite, Luna. The very person of the King was a pawn in these struggles. Without at all being a complete list, the following gives some idea of the sorry state of affairs: in 1420 the King was seized by Prince Enrique, son of Fernando I of Aragon, and the grandees; in 1425 the Kings of Aragon and Navarre were in open opposition to the King of Castile; in 1427, don Álvaro de Luna was exiled from court, but returned the following year (this was only one of at least three instances when

he was forced from the court); in 1435 the King of Navarre and his brother, Prince Enrique, besieged the King in
Escalona; in 1443 the King was virtually a prisoner of
the nobles in Tordesillas. The culmination, although not the
end of the turbulences, came in 1445, when the civil strife
reached the point of producing a pitched battle at Olmedo.
The leaders of the revolt were the King of Navarre and his
brother, Prince Enrique, and other ancient enemies of
Luna's. On this particular occasion Juan II and don Álvaro
were supported by the Crown Prince (the future Enrique
IV, who on many other occasions was allied with the nobles against his own father), the Counts of Haro and Alva,
Iñigo Lópoz de Mendoza (also frequently opposed to Luna)
and Lope de Barrientos, among others. The battle took place
on May 29, 1445, and was a clear victory for the King
of Castile. As a result, the King of Navarre and his brother
withdrew to Aragon, and the latter died shortly afterward
in Calatayud. When the news of his death reached Castile,
don Álvaro de Luna, at the King's behest, was elected to
succeed him as Grand Master of the Order of Santiago. He
was now at the height of his wealth and power. Iñigo López
de Mendoza was rewarded for his loyalty at this battle by
being made Marquis of Santillana and Count of the Real.

For the account of the battle of Olmedo we again have
recourse to the *Crónica de don Álvaro de Luna,* a really
invaluable source of information about all aspects of warfare in fifteenth century Spain. The author treats it, essen-
tially, in four stages: (1) the description of the gallant
knights, rich in color and detail about clothing, (2) the
arrangement of the battle lines, (3) the battle proper, with
stress on the valor of Luna and (4) the listing of casualties
and prisoners.

*How the Constable arranged his squadron and the lines of
his vanguard, when he was about to go forth to strike.*

Now the squadrons of the King of Castile were drawn up in
this manner: the Constable, who held the vanguard, had very good
soldiers and knights, noble and skilled and accustomed to war, and
both they and their horses were well and elegantly armed. For wars
had been so continuous in Castile that the endeavors of all were
directed solely to maintaining their weapons in order and their
horses well selected. So true was this that you could scarcely find
in all of the Constable's army a person whose horse was uncovered,

and even the horses' necks were protected with steel chain-mail. And all those young, noble knights of the Constable's household, and many others, were richly equipped, for some had diverse emblems painted on their horses' armor and wore gifts from their ladies as pennants over their helmets.

Others had heavy chains with gold and silver bells around their horses' necks; and there were some who wore bullions set with pearls and precious stones as edgings for their helmets. There were others who carried small bucklers, richly ornamented with wonderful symbols and devices. No small diversity did they display in the crest of their sallets and helmets, for some wore crests of wild beasts, others variegated panaches, and there were those who used feathers, both as crests for their helmets and as crownpieces for their horses. Nor were there lacking people who sported plumes like wings, which extended down their backs. Some went in rough harness; others wore jackets overlaid with plates over their armor, and others richly embroidered surcoats. So went all the Constable's troops and most of those who gathered for this war. As it was already late, and the sun was shining directly on them, and their trappings were polished and their armor gleamed, they all presented a fine appearance.

These select troops were arranged by the Constable in this fashion: he ordered Juan Carrillo, the *adelantado* of Cazorla, to go ahead of his men at arms with the light cavalry, riding with high stirrups, and he sent his retainer, Juan Fernández, a man skilled in warfare, with him. They were commanded to strike against the cavalry of the opposing side. The Constable himself entered the battle with a squadron of well chosen and well equipped men at arms, as we have said, in which were many noble knights and gentlemen of his household. For included that day were don Pero de Luna, his natural son, a young knight, well disposed and daring in arms, who worked hard to emulate his father in skill and courage; Pero Sarmiento, the son of Diego Pérez Sarmiento, the King's chief steward and a member of his council; Pero García, the Marshal of Castile; Alfonso Pérez de Vivero, the King's Chief Purser and a member of his council; and Carlos de Arellano and many other knights.

The Constable ordered a square of fifty picked men at arms to precede this squadron to pierce the enemy before him. The captains of this unit were Fernando de Ferrera (the eldest son of Marshal Pero García) and Luis de la Cerda, two young knights famed for their virtue, who from childhood had been reared in the Constable's house. Because they were close relatives, very fond of one another, and boon companions, the Constable never wished to separate them in the pursuit of war. He ordered two more squares of eighty or a hundred men each to move on the right hand of his squadron. In the first were don Alfonso Carrillo, Bishop of Siguenza, who later became Archbishop of Toledo, and his brother, Pero de Acuña, cousins of the Constable's and of his household. Behind this came another square of eighty or a hundred men, whose captains were Juan de Guzmán, knight commander of Calatrava, and Doctor Pero González Dávila, Lord of Villatoro and Navamorcuende and a member of the King's council.

On the left hand he ordered two other squadrons to march. They were captained by Juan de Luna, the King's chief guard, who was a nephew of the Constable's and married to his natural daughter, and Gutierre Quixada, Lord of Villagarcia, and another knight from Galicia named Rodrigo de Moscoso. All these knights belonged to the Constable's household and were very eager to serve and honor him, as they proved that day. There must have been some seven hundred and eighty men at arms in the squadron and units of the Constable, and two hundred light cavalrymen. Behind this squadron of the Constable's, and placed slightly to the right, came don Fernán Álvarez de Toledo, the Count of Alva, and Iñigo López de Mendoza with their troops in one squadron. Also behind the Constable's squadron, but a little to the left, was the Prince's squadron and that of the Grand Master of Alcántara. Then came the main squadron, in which was the King.

In such a manner were the squadrons of the King of Castile, the Prince his son, and the Constable and other grandees who were with him arranged that day.

How the King of Navarre and the Prince arranged their squadrons, of those who came to strike against the squadron of the Constable.

The King of Navarre and the Prince arranged their troops in this wise: in the squadron of the King of Navarre came his men with his standard, and the standard of the Count of Medinaceli with his troops, and the Count of Castro with his squadron. In the squadron of the Prince Enrique, Grand Master of Santiago, were the troops of don Fadrique, the Admiral of Castile, don Alfonso Pimentel, Count of Benavente, with his units, don Enrique, the brother of the Admiral, Rodrigo Manrique, Commander of Segura, Pero Juárez de Quiñones, Juan de Tovar, and Diego de Benavides. These people were in the forefront, and as they knew that the Constable's squadron was very thick and had the choicest warriors and those most accustomed to war, they decided that all of them would direct their standards and squadrons against the Constable's, and so they did, when the time came to strike.

How the King had a pitched battle with the King of Navarre, the Prince and their followers, and how the Constable was the first to strike against them.

Since the Constable was in the van and was a skillful and knowledgeable knight, learned in the ways of war, he recognized that the troops of Olmedo were coming to seize a high hill that was between the lines of battle. He therefore ordered the *adelantado* Juan Carrillo to ride with the cavalry to take it. He also commanded his men at arms to move forward in rank to that hill. The *adelantado* and the cavalry moved to carry out his orders, but since the opposing troops were numerous and had reached the hill before the Constable's soldiers, his light cavalry had to leave off, and the men at arms of both sides arrived there. As Prince Enrique and the squadrons previously named saw the Constable's troops, they pressed forward to strike, all together, as they had agreed. These were the Prince, the Admiral, the Count of Benavente, don Enrique, the Admiral's brother, Pero Juárez de Quiñones and Rodrigo Manrique, with their squadrons, who must have numbered fourteen hundred soldiers in all.

When the Constable saw them all coming to attack his squadron, he sent his men straight towards them; they lowered their lances over their arms and, shouting "Castile, Castile," pressed to the attack. The first blows were delivered by them. As the troops on both sides were very eager —the King's men to serve him and receive death for his sake, and the enemy to offend and do him injury— they went at each other with such fury and broke their lances on one another so strenuously that many bit the earth, some wounded and others knocked down with their horses. After they had broken their lances, they drew forth their swords and began to strike with might and main, and those on the ground who were able to get up killed the horses from under those who had unseated them, and did each other as much harm as possible; the more the wounds increased among them, the more heated became the battle.

The King, seeing his men engaged in combat, approached with his squadrons, urging them on and sending word to fight and increase their effort, for he was there to help them whenever it might be necessary, as was the Prince, his son. Now the squadrons of the Constable and the Prince and the Admiral and those other knights had broken through each other and were wheeling around to mingle and strike and do as much injury as they could. As the enmity between them was great and hatred gave them added strength, they hurled themselves at each other and their horses collided chest to chest, and they fell to earth heavily and others passed right over the fallen and ground them down. Some snatched the armor from the heads of others, and others struck them down with powerful blows.

So great was the drive of battle, and the Prince's soldiers and those with them pressed so hard against the Constable and his banner that they killed his standard bearer's horse. He fell and his banner was hurled to the ground, but it was lifted up again at once, for nearby were many good and noble knights who succored him well. The battle was very stubborn and hard fought on both sides. But the Constable was everywhere, bravely and quickly urging his men on, sometimes as captain and other times fighting personally, helping here and there, wherever he understood he could best avail them. Such was his activity that all his men saw him before them and took heart to do well even though the Constable was already wounded in the thigh from a lance blow. He kept the wound concealed for a long time and did not cease fighting because of it, nor did any of his men realize that he was injured.

The struggle was most bitter and obstinate there, for courageous knights, well skilled in warfare, were fighting on both sides, and the fervor of soldiers and captains of both parties was concentrated at that point. The battle was so intense that for a long time the outcome was in doubt, for it was impossible to tell which side would emerge victorious. But as the victory of battles is in the hands of God, He, seeing the just cause and truth of the King of Castile and the serious offences that the others had committed against his royal excellence, and how the King of Navarre had broken the truce, was pleased that the King of Castile should be the victor in this battle, and the King of Navarre, the Prince and all those with them should be vanquished.

When they could no longer hold out against the terrible blows that the Constable and his troops were raining down on them, the King of Navarre, Prince Enrique, the Admiral, the Count of Benavente and all the rest turned their backs and put to flight, routed and driven from the field. The King of Castile's troops pressed on, wounding and capturing many, shouting, "Return, you evil traitors, faithless to the King who did you so many favors. Seek not a shameful death in flight; return and receive death at our hands, and feel the steel of his justice."

They gave no answer, but fled as fast as they could; and the King's men pressed the pursuit, wounding, capturing and beating them down almost to the city of Olmedo.

Concerning those who where killed, captured and wounded by the Constable's men in this battle.

In this battle, many soldiers of the King of Navarre, the Prince and the rest were killed, wounded and destroyed, and a goodly number —more than three hundred— were captured. Among the prisoners in particular were don Enrique and Fernando de Quiñones; the latter later died of the wounds he had received. Also captured were Diego and Rodrigo de Mendoza, the brothers of Pedro de Mendoza, García de Losana, Juan Bernal, Diego de Londoño, the son of Sancho de Londoño, Marshal of the King of Navarre, Rodrigo Dávalos, grandson of Ruy López Dávalos, one time Constable of Castile, Diego Carrillo, son of Alfonso Carrillo, and many other knights and squires.

Also seized by the Constable's troops were the standards of the Prince, the Admiral, the Count of Benavente, don Enrique and Rodrigo Manrique, and the ensigns who carried them were taken prisoner. Admiral don Fadrique was captured too, but a squire who held him prisoner concealed and went off with him, because of the great promises that the Admiral made to him. This was possible because night had fallen by the time the battle was over. In this combat the Prince received a wound in his arm, near the hand, from which he died. A stroke of fortune and guile liberated Pero Juárez de Quiñones from a squire of the Constable's company who was taking him prisoner, for Pero Juárez de Quiñones said to him:

"Squire, I am badly wounded, and I beg you to remove this helmet from my head, for it is killing me."

The squire, believing him, handed over the sword he was carrying, to hold while he removed his armor, and Pero Juárez, seeing his chance, struck the squire a tremendous blow on the face with the sword, left him thus impeded, put spurs to his horse and fled as fast as he was able, saving himself on that occasion. If it had not been so late, the Constable's men would have wreaked even greater havoc on the troops of the King of Navarre, the Prince and their allies; but nightfall kept more of them from being destroyed.

(Gonzalo Chacón, *Crónica de don Álvaro de Luna,* chapters 53 to 56.)

THE SIEGE OF ATIENZA

Another type of military action was siege warfare. In the year following the battle of Olmedo, the town of Atienza was besieged by the forces of the King of Castile because it was still being held by Rodrigo de Robledo, a vassal of King Juan of Navarre, with some two hundred and fifty knights and five hundred foot-soldiers. The town finally surrendered after two months, and the King of Castile entered it on August 12, 1446. He ordered the walls broken down and the entire town set to the torch. The following passage, again from the chronicle relating the affairs of don Álvaro de Luna, covers only one incident in the siege, but it is a typical episode of this type of warfare. The picture of the Constable-Grand Master proceeding to the scene of battle on a mule is especially intriguing.

*How the Grand Master [don Álvaro de Luna] entered the
suburb of the Horses' Gate, to close up some wells from
which the townspeople were supplied with water, and
about the battle that took place over them.*

The King and the Grand Master had learned from certain
people in the city of Atienza who had come over to him how the
townspeople were lacking water and were sustained only by that
which they took from some wells in the suburb of the Horses' Gate,
especially from one they had next to the town gate. The King was
therefore very desirous that the soldiers he was awaiting would
arrive, so he could take that suburb, for by capturing it, they could
take away their well water and sap from the lower part of the suburb the well they had by the town gate. The soldiers that the
King had there were few, as we have said, and to take that suburb
required a strong force of crossbowmen, for it was very near the
city and right under its summit; nevertheless, the Grand Master of
Santiago, seeing the great service that would be done the King and
the great harm that the townspeople would receive if that suburb
were captured and the wells closed up, and thinking not of hardships
nor fearing danger, was willing to attempt anything he thought
would be to the King's service.

On Thursday, the day before the Feast of St. John in June, the
Grand Master armed himself and had his men arm, those who were
billeted outside the suburbs in the encampment, for those in the
trenches had enough to do guarding their barricades. Almost all
of the knights, retainers and relatives of the Grand Master, went
with him that day, but they took along few crossbowmen, for the
crossbowmen who were there had been ordered by the King to be
distributed along the trenches of the soldiers who were set up in
the main suburb, and in order not to take those bowmen away, the
Grand Master took very few with him. The Grand Master proceeded
with this force to the Horses' Gate suburb and entered it; for the
town forces did not tarry there, but took refuge in the upper part
of the city. The Grand Master went with his men to take up a
position at a church that overlooked the entire suburb, a church
called St. Anthony's which was very near the city gate and had an
entrance facing the suburb.

The Grand Master came in through the suburb with his men and went up with them to that church, although they were endangered during the ascent by many arrows, artillery pieces, culverins, stones thrown by hand or slings, and missile throwers. Some were wounded while going up, but nevertheless the Grand Master encouraged his men and continued with them until he got them to the entrance of the church. Those who went inside the church discovered that the entire wall facing the city rampart was knocked down and broken open, for the town's forces had torn it down the night before so that soldiers could not take shelter in the church and it was unroofed overhead, and was so close to the city gate that there was not a stone's throw between them.

After he arrived there with the knights of his household and a few others who went along, the Grand Master talked with them, asking who they thought should be put in charge to stay with the force in that church; because, if they were there, the main well by the city gate could be quickly sapped and the people inside would be completely surrounded, which they had not been until then. The knights of the Grand Master's household, and the others, each replied that his grace should not order any of them to undertake the responsibility of remaining with troops in such a place, where they would be exposed to manifest danger and harm without being able to do anything to the King's service or his, or to their honor. But each and all said that if his grace ordered them to stay, without being in charge of other men, they would remain, although they knew well that they would be in a position of losing their lives without having the chance to do well.

The Grand Master, who was a very courageous knight and a stout-hearted captain, was displeased by the reply he got from his men, and began to argue with them and castigate the weakness of their hearts with harsh words, saying he had never met less courageous knighthood, and that he himself would remain there and thus they would be forced to stay with him even if they did not wish to. And he ordered his bed brought at once. The knights who were with the Grand Master had seen the church and knew that the wall facing the city wall was demolished and the roof off, and the church yard outside was uphill toward the city, and the wall was pulled down and levelled with the church roof against the city wall; thus they could not remain in the church except to their injury. They showed the Grand Master the church and the things that moved them to tell him he ought not order them to remain in such a place; finally the Grand Master recognized that they were right in declining to stay there.

Then the Grand Master ordered them to remain where they were, for he wanted to go seek out another, safer place to set up. And he rode on a mule, armed as he was, for he was tired; all that morning he had gone with his armor on and on foot, having them construct barricades around the church. He went down a little in the suburb to another small church that was there, and ordered certain barricades and palisades set up in the middle of the suburb. He left those knights in the upper church while he was having the barricades built lower down, so the trenches would be in less danger. While these things were going on, a majority of the town's forces, seeing those men so close to the city wall, right under them and at a great disadvantage, gathered together and armed themselves. And while they were getting armed, the men who were on top of the walls kept raining down many stones, arrows, and artillery missiles, and wounded some of the few crossbowmen that the Grand Master had brought along, for they were not wearing armor.

For this reason, all of the crossbowmen they had there quietly and secretly withdrew and soon returned to camp and some went back injured. So the knights were left waiting and suffering there with the men at arms. The sun was very strong and the heat intense, so they all suffered on two accounts: from the weather, which was very hot, and from the townsmen, who were wounding them with many stones and arrows. The Grand Master was down below, suffering no less hardship, arranging and hurrying on the barricades and preparing trenches for the men. The soldiers of the town sallied forth in a body, and with the greatest fury they could muster and a loud clamor fell upon the knights at the church, and with them came a strong force of archers, who began to shoot into those at the church.

The fighting was very bitter, for those at the church were especially chosen men of good merit, and some were young knights, retainers of the Grand Master's. They stationed themselves along two streets on either side of the church and began to fight valiantly, but the forces above had such an advantage over them that they were inflicting great harm with little danger to themselves. And when they realized that the Grand Master's men had no crossbow-men, they cast aside their big leather shields, loaded up with rocks and hurled them at the forces by the church. The city crossbowmen came so close to aim their shots that the men by the church rushed them and cut their bow strings. The men in the streets opposed the descent of the city forces with lance thrusts, and fought fiercely with their swords, until they clashed head on with the city forces and began a hand-to-hand combat. Many of the Grand Master's knights were wounded by the enemy, both by rocks and by arrows, but they brought such ardor to the fight that some of them had been wounded for a long while without even realizing it, so eager were they to do themselves honor.

Now the coats-of-mail of the Grand Master's knights were all coming undone; pieces were falling off here and there and others were disconnected and out of place. Some of the city men had already climbed up on the church and set it afire; others were coming along other streets to cut off all those knights, and they could have done it, since there were so many of them and they had the advantage.

When the Grand Master, who was arranging the barricades lower down, heard that his men were fighting and learned that the knights he had left at the church were completely cut off and hard pressed on all sides by the forces of the city, he was sorely grieved; but, as he was a valiant and daring captain, he hurriedly grabbed his helmet, put it on his head (for he had on all his other armor) and mounted a mule to go up the slope, in order to arrive more rested for the fighting.

Although he was alone when he began to ascend the hill, he began to gather up some of his knights who were retreating from above, urging them on and rallying them around himself. He ordered his trumpets sounded, arrived very quickly at the church, and went along some side streets to reach the heights above the church. When he got there, the two sides were so mixed up and close to each other that he could not make out the city forces, except by seeing that they were hurling many rocks and arrows. The Grand Master began to urge on his knights and to inspire courage in them, with the result that they pressed the attack all together with him. When the city troops saw that, they began to withdraw. Someone among them began to shout loudly that they should return to the city, for the troops from the trenches in the other suburbs were fighting with the city's defenders and were about to break through. It was true that the knights from the trenches were fighting with the city forces, for the King had sent the command, so that the many men who had rushed there would withdraw, seeing themselves combatted on another side. Therefore all the people of Atienza withdrew to the city.

Then the Grand Master gathered together all his knights, placed them before him, and went down to the lower area. Thus did he deliver those knights that day so that they were not lost, which had been very likely; and it was a great victory to keep his men from being defeated. Now, when the Grand Master was descending, Pedro de Luxán arrived with about ten knights that were with the King.

After the enemy had withdrawn to the city, the Grand Master had all the wells in that suburb blocked up, and wanted to go back to fixing the barricades and remain there himself with his men. But all the knights with him begged him not to try it; rather, since he had delivered them in such a fashion that day, they said that he should go to the King, who was alone and did not know the outcome, and that he could better arrange that deed another day, with stronger defenses than he then had. Because they insisted so much, the Grand Master gathered his men and returned to the King.

The King was very pleased when he learned there were no deaths among his men, for when he saw the struggle joined, he thought for sure that many of his troops would be killed. But it pleased God that none of the King's men, nor the Grand Master's, died in that battle, although there were many wounded who were in danger of dying. Among the wounded were Martín de Alarcón, Juan Fernández Galindo, Knight Commander of the Order of Santiago, and many others.

The Grand Master was very grieved for all those who were wounded, and especially for this Juan Fernández, because his wound was very dangerous, and because he was a very brave man and of great counsel in deeds of war. And since he had served the Grand Master well in many wars, he had been given that Knight Commandery and had been done other favors. The Grand Master, after he had gathered his men, returned with the King to camp.

(Gonzalo Chacón, *Crónica de don Alvaro de Luna,* chapter 65)

KNIGHTHOOD

A Definition of a Knight

The ideal of chivalry was very much alive in the fifteenth century. Serious works were written on the subject; the learned Bishop of Burgos, Alfonso de Cartagena, replied in an erudite letter to a query of the Marquis of Santillana concerning the oath that a knight should take, and he composed a long treatise on the history and meaning of knighthood, the *Doctrinal de caballeros* (*Catechism of knights*). Rather than use learned, theoretical works of this nature, however, I have preferred to present two passages from the chronicle of a true and living knight. This is the *Victorial*, by Gutierre Díez de Games. It is a panegyrical biography of Pero Niño, Count of Buelna, or perhaps more accurately, a partial life of Pero Niño combined with a doctrine of chivalry and examples of great knights. The hero was an important personage during the time of the Constable Ruy López Dávalos, the Regent Prince Fernando, and, ultimately, don Alvaro de Luna. He lived from about 1378 to 1453, although the chronicle goes only to 1446, perhaps because the author died around that time. The latter must have been approximately the same age as Pero Niño and was his standard bearer in battle and constant companion in his many adventures. The nucleus of the *Victorial* covers the years 1403 to 1410, from the time Pero Niño set out against pirates in the Mediterranean, through his adventures, amorous and chivalric, in France, his campaigns against the English coast, his return to Castile and his marriage to doña Beatriz de Portugal (see later, the section on marriage and love). The chronicle presents throughout a curious mingling of the real and historical with the literary and imaginative, a confluence that is not always skillfully accomplished. In spite of its faults, however, the work has great human interest, due to the impression it creates of being an eye-witness acount.

The first passage, a definition of knighthood, is from the eighth and final chapter of the introduction. It begins as a rather conventional portrait of the ideal knight, includes a well-known story from Spanish history, and ends on a high note of realism. The lively and convincing picture of the life of a fighting man and the hardships he endures stamps the author as one who knew whereof he wrote.

Now it is fitting to tell what a knight is, whence he takes this name of knight, how a knight should be, so that he may truly deserve to be called a knight, and what benefit a good knight brings to the country in which he lives. I tell you, first of all, that "knight" is used for a man who habitually rides a horse. A person who usually rides another type of mount is not a knight, nor is the person who rides a horse a knight, just for that reason. The one who can truthfully be called a knight is he who carries out the duties.

They were not chosen to ride asses or mules, nor were weak, timorous or cowardly men chosen, but robust and strong men, fearless and brave. Therefore, there is no animal more befitting a knight than a good horse. One finds that some horses were as loyal to their masters in times of danger as if they were men. Good horses are strong, eager, swift and loyal; so that a good man on a good horse will do more than ten other men, perhaps even more than a hundred, will do in an hour of battle. Therefore, this type of person should be called a knight.

What should a good knight be? He should be noble. What is noble and nobility? His heart should be governed by virtues. With what virtues? With those four I have talked about before. These four virtues are sisters, and are so bound to each other that he who has one, has all, and he who lacks one, lacks all the others. A good and virtuous knight should be wise and prudent, a fair judge, temperate and circumspect, strong and brave; along with these qualities, he should have great faith in God and hope in His glory and that he will receive reward for the good he may do, and he should have charity and loving-kindness for people.

What profit does the good knight bring? I tell you that because of good knights the king and his kingdom are honored and feared, defended and protected. I tell you that the king is safer when he sends a good knight with an army and entrusts to him a great deed, either on land or sea. I tell you that a king without good knights is like a man without hands or feet.

We have an example in that King Alfonso, who rejected the knights and committed many excesses against them, on the advice of a Jew; and because of the lack of knights, he was defeated at the battle which is called Alarcos. Afterwards, the King, seeing from where the harm came, was reconciled with the knights and came to the battle against the King of Benamarin and Miramomalin, and the King Bursaban, and the King of Morocco, and the King of Tremecen and many other kings and against so many Moors that they could not be counted. The King was afraid that some of his knights would not help him as well as they ought, because of what he had done to them. And it happened that, going into battle at the third hour, the King saw a white gonfalon with black markings fleeing, and thought it was the Lord of Lara, and said: "Now I see that the knights are deserting me in the battle."

Andrés Boca de Medina, the most powerful and richest commoner in Castile, happened to be near the King, and to encourage him, he said: "Do not believe, sire, that the knights are fleeing. It is only we commoners who are running away." So it was, for only the banner of Madrid fled. And it pleased God to help them and all fought well and were victorious. It is even true that the King waited five days for a good knight, for him alone, because he knew what kind of a person he was. It is a grand thing and should be held in high esteem, that such a great army, in which there were three kings (those of Castile, Aragon and Navarre) waited for a single knight and did not begin the battle until he arrived; and the one who waited for him had seen him before in other cases of need and knew who he was. This was the great battle that is known as the Navas de Tolosa. Even though there may be many knights in an army, it happens that a battle is won, or a city gained (and sometimes even a kingdom) because of one good knight.

Not all those who ride horses are knights, nor are all those that kings dub really knights. They have the name, but they do not carry out the duties of warfare. For noble knighthood is the most honorable office of all. Everyone wishes to rise to that honor; they wear the clothes and bear the title, but they do not keep the rule. They are not knights, but false and conceited people. The habit does not make the monk, but the monk the habit. Many are called and few chosen.

There is not, nor should there be, among all occupations, any as honored as this. For people of ordinary callings eat their bread with leisure, wear delicate clothing, have well prepared meals and soft, perfumed beds; they lie down safe and get up without fear; they enjoy themselves in fine dwellings with their wives and children and are waited on at their will; they grow fat necks and get big bellied; they wish themselves well by taking care of themselves and staying comfortable. What reward or honor do they deserve? None at all.

Knights, in war, eat their bread with affliction; their delights are aches and sweat; one good day among many bad ones. They face all hardships, they swallow many fears, they go through many dangers, they hazard their lives to live or die. Mouldy bread or hardtack; badly cooked food; sometimes they have something to eat, and sometimes nothing. Little or no wine. Water from pools or wine skins. Their armor on, loaded down with iron; the enemy within sight. Bad lodgings and worse beds. A shelter of tatters or leaves; a bad bed, bad sleep.

Look out, there!

Who goes there?

To arms! To arms!

When they lie down to sleep, alarms; at dawn, trumpets.

Ride, ride!

Soldiers in sight!

Spies, sentries, look-outs, scouts, advance guards, guards, second guards.

There they are, there they are!

They're not so many.

Yes they are.

Go there!

Come this way!

You come here!

You go there!

News! News!

They are coming back injured.

They are not bringing anything!

Yes they are!

Let's go! Let's go!
Let's stay!
Let's go!

Such is their task, a life of hardship, far from all pleasure. As for those on the sea, there is nothing equal to their bad life. I could not finish telling in a whole day their wretchedness and hardship. Thus have been told, through the things I have said, the honor and the great favors from kings that knights deserve.

> (Gutierre Díez de Games, *El Victorial*, chapter 8.)

The Education of a Knight

The second selection from the *Victorial* is from the first of the three parts into which the body of the work is divided. This first division tells about the lineage, youthful years and first marriage of the hero. The passage presented deals with his education. In reality, it must be taken as the ideal education for knighthood, as seen by the author, rather than as a true account of Pero Niño's upbringing. The figure of the "wise and able man" who instructs him, the presentation of a series of admonitions and exhortations and the emphasis on religious duty are all typical of the medieval didactic attitude, and seem like late echos of Juan Manuel or Ramon Llull. The strange scorn for formal education is but a pose, and is given the lie by the very erudition that the author displays throughout the work.

When Pero Niño was ten years old, he was given to be reared and trained to a wise and able man, who was to teach and instruct him in all the good customs that a good and noble gentleman should have. And he taught him in this way:

"My son, take heed that you are of great lineage, and that the wheel of the world, which is never still nor lets things stay in good estate, brought down your very honored line, and made the great small and the lofty poor and low. You must struggle and work to return to that estate, and even surpass in grandeur and nobility those from whom you are descended; for it is nothing wonderful for a man to resemble his father in maintaining that estate that he was left, for he found it already earned, but it is very praiseworthy for him to exceed all those from whom he comes and gain greater dignity.

My son, take careful note of my words, instruct your heart in my sayings and retain them, for later you will understand them. It is not necessary for a person who is to learn and use this art of chivalry to spend a long time in a school of letters. What you have left to learn about it will come with time, if you practice it a little.

Above all, know God, then yourself, and then others. Know God through faith. What is faith? Faith is a very firm certainty about something unseen, an argument of the spirit with the ordinary flow of reason. Know the substance through the accidents. Know Him who created you and gave you being. Know God through His creations and the marvels He made. Understand and know His great power, for He made the heaven and earth and the sea, and all the things that are therein.

He created the angels in light and adorned and embellished the heavens with many beautiful stars. He created the sun and the moon, and commanded the sun to shine by day and the moon to shine by night; and He adorned and filled the earth with many diverse plants, of trees and herbs, and He stocked it with animals of many different shapes, and He created the great whales and many different fish in the sea, and He created birds in the water and placed them in the air. And note how He put a limit to the sea, that it does not go beyond a certain point, so as not to destroy the land.

My son, see how the sun rises in the east and sets in the west, and returns whence it came, and how the skies are, and the sea, and the earth, which is secured over the sea. And all the things He made obey Him and do not go beyond His commands and the limits that He first set them. Consider how He created man in His image, and how He put him in a Paradise of ease, and how He ordered him to serve, love and fear Him and be obedient to His command, and he would live forever in happiness and perfect pleasure and would never die nor suffer pain or travail; how He put under man's command and power all the things that He created in the sea and on the land.

And see how wretched man was deceived, and sinned through his weakness; he trespassed the command of God, for which reason divine justice took place and condemned him to the death of the body and soul, and he was expelled from Paradise into the desert of this world, to suffer and to die. Where he was free, he became the subject and captive of death, and he left us, his children, in that same captivity, obligated to sin.

My son, love and keep Him, who threw down from the heights of heaven to the depths of the abyss, from glory into suffering, from brightness to perpetual shadow and darkness, where he became the devil and prince of death, that excellent and beautiful angel, full of glory, who in his pride said: "I shall place my seat in the north, over the heavens, and I shall be equal to the most high Creator."

Love Him who not only deigned to assume our flesh, but became as humble as a servant and suffered for us, and took our burden upon His shoulders, and freed us from the power of the devil and from the cruel dominion under which we were, through our subjection to sin.

My beloved son, believe and hold firmly what holy Mother Church believes and holds; I know of nothing that should separate or move you from her. What shall I say to you? You have been born in the holy faith and regenerated in the water of the Holy Spirit. If it is necessary for you to fight with your body alone against anyone who might say that the holy Catholic faith is not so, you are obligated to do it; this is good chivalry, the best that any knight can perform, to fight for his religion and faith, and all the more so, being in the right. And if by chance you fall into the hands of enemies of our holy Catholic faith, and they wish to make you deny it, you must be ready to suffer all the tortures that may befall you, for if one keeps and confesses the holy faith of Jesus Christ until death, in such a holy battle, as I have said before, he who dies is called the victor and the slayer is called the vanquished.

Take example from the knight St. James, all of whose limbs and joints, from fingers to toes, were hacked off one by one, but they could never make him deny Jesus Christ; rather, he remained firm, like a good knight. This is good, triumphant chivalry; in this way does one gain the golden crown that God promises to the victors. Let no one say in such a moment: "Oh what a hard thing is death! I shall deny now and do what they command me, for, since I do it not willingly, I shall recant later, when there is opportunity."

I tell you that he who gives in will not emerge victorious, nor can he who puts his foot in the net withdraw it when he wishes. Friends are known in time of fortune. But having firm faith and hoping in the reward, sufferings are sweet. Consider that the suffering of hell is harsher than physical suffering. This pain passes quickly, but that of hell lasts forever.

What more shall I tell you, my son? Do not believe nor engage in subtle arguments concerning religion. What your intelligence may not comprehend or attain, believe on faith; for if there were some proof for faith, there would be no merit in it. God did not create you to judge His deeds, but to be obedient to His commandments. Know the great grandeur of God over you. How can the thing created, weak and mortal, know the infinite, without grace? The holy Catholic faith is already purified like gold that, put into the fiery oven seven times —not only seven, but seventy thousand times seven— comes out more brilliant each time.

My son, carry out all your deeds with God, keep His commandments, do His precepts, guard His churches, honor His feasts and their mysteries, and He will keep and honor you. Entrust your deeds to Him, seek great things from Him, for He is very rich and will give you what is best for you. Place your hope in Him, for without Him nothing is accomplished. What is done without Him is nothing; what is done through Him is living and lasting.

My son, bend your ear to the petition of the poor, hear him, answer him peacefully and gently, and give him charity; deliver him who suffers injury out of the hand of the proud. Make worthy prayers to God and read books. Keep His works in mind; consider that when we pray we are talking to God, and when we read He is talking with us.

My son, do not believe those people who will tell you that they will make you see and know your fortune; for they will tell you that you are to be very great, and are to attain this or that, and of everything they tell you, nothing will come to pass. If you believed them, you would lose His name; and engaging in vain hopes, you would waste the time needed for the things of your honor and estate. Believe that God made you without you, and that without you He will save you. Beware of believing in false prophecies, such as those of Merlin and the rest, or of having any trust in them; for I tell you truly that these things were schemed up and brought forth by clever and adroit men, to gain favor and power with kings and great men, and to gain from them, and keep them under their will with these vain hopes, while they make their profit.

If you will notice, when a new king comes, they make a new Merlin. They say that the king is to pass over the sea and destroy the power of the Moors, and win the holy city, and become Emperor. And then we see that it happens as it pleases God. So did they speak of past kings and will speak of those to come. What God refused to reveal to His chosen ones, sinners pretend to know: for all true prophets spoke only to the purpose of the two comings of Jesus Christ, the first, with humility and poverty, the last, with power and majesty. After that, all were silent, for after the coming of Jesus Christ, they are no longer needed. Merlin was a good and very learned man. He was not the son of the Devil, as some say, for the Devil, who is spirit, cannot engender; he can provoke sinful things, for such is his function. He is an incorporeal substance and cannot beget a corporeal one.

But Merlin, with the great wisdom he acquired, wished to know more than was suitable for him, and was deceived by the Devil, who showed him many things he should say. Some of these came true, for this is the way of the Devil, or even of anyone who knows how to deceive: throw out some truth, in order to be believed by the person he wishes to ensnare. Thus, in that region of England, he said some things in which there was some truth, but in many others he was wrong.

Some people who now wish to say certain things, compose them and say that Merlin spoke them. But all things, past, present and future, are in the presence of God alone. Who is that person who knows the will of God in the things that are to come? Or does man know more than God? This is false.

Take note that God made many things, but He did not make any that could go against His power. See how Jesus Christ replied to His disciples, when they asked Him about some things to come and about the Antichrist: It is not meet that you should know the hour and the moment that God appointed in His wisdom.

Of this much can you be certain and know what is to come; that after the summer comes the winter, and it behooves us to prepare for the winter with warm and sheltered houses, and firewood and victuals, for the season that is hard and mean, when you cannot get them; and during the winter provide yourself with the things necessary for it. Take note of the sailor, who during good weather prepares for the bad, and during bad weather gets ready and awaits the good. This is good divination and knowledge that is profitable.

Also, my son, beware of the deceptions of men who say that they will make you two or four *doblas* (coins) from one, or that they will make you silver from rock and gold from copper, and that in this way they will make your wealth and importance increase, and that you can be the greatest man there ever was in your family, and that you will be able to make liberal grants and get ahead of your rivals. They will give you a deceitful demonstration to make you believe it, and if you fall for it, in the end you will find yourself poor and all your wealth wasted. I tell you that for this they seek out greedy and not very bright men, who lose their wealth and spend their lives mocked and humiliated among people.

Adhere to the company of the good and you will be one of them. Beware the company of the wicked, for your nature will secretly steal from theirs. Be temperate in your eating, drinking and sleeping. Do not follow your will in things that can bring you harm. He who does not know that the will is the enemy of intelligence is very stupid. Plato says that we should not always go with our will, but against our will, for going against the will is a second way of going, which is good and is of the nature of the soul, which controls the body and the senses. Then the body is held back, controlled and set right by the soul, which embellishes it with fasts and prayers, chastity and good customs. If the body is abandoned and given over to its will, it gives itself up to anger, lust, avarice and pride, and other sins that are of the nature of the earth, which governs the body, with the other elements...

My son, do not lower your noble person to frequenting wicked women, for they do not love and wish to be loved; connexion with them is a shortening of life, corruption of virtues and transgression of the laws of God.

My son, when you are to speak before men, first pass [*your words*] over the file of your intelligence, before they come to your tongue. Consider that the tongue is a tree, and has its roots in the heart, and the tongue is the external part. Note that while you are speaking, others are examining your words, as you examine theirs when they speak. Therefore, say reasonable things; if not, it would be better for you to be silent. Through speech is knowledge known, through intelligence, wisdom, and in the word, truth and learning; firmness through deeds. Oh, if he who should not speak would be still, and if he who should not keep quiet would speak! Truth would never be contradicted.

My son, beware of avarice if you wish to have power over yourself; otherwise, you will be a slave, for as the accumulation of wealth increases, so increase the multitude of cares. Take note; if you wish to have what you desire, desire what you can have. Judge no man by what he has wrought in his fortune, but judge him by what he is in intelligence and virtue. For the honor of animals, clothing and mounts is the honor of metals, it is of the earth; but intelligence and virtues belong to the soul.

Do not have vassals merely for what you can get from them, but hold them all as friends and let them serve you with what is rightfully your due. With a gentle word love endures in hearts; a sweet word multiplies friends and allays enemies; a pleasing tongue suffices in a good man. Note that in the time of your prosperity many will pay you homage.

Let your adviser be one among a thousand. If you have a friend of the season, have him, but do not believe him easily nor too quickly, because his friendship is according to the season. If your friend remains unswerving with you, he will be as another self to you. Avoid your enemies; do not trust in them. Lead such a life among men that, if you die, they will mourn for you, and if you go away, they will long for your company. If you see a sick person, lacking wits, do not mock him, but ask yourself if you are of the same nature. If you are healthy, give thanks to God. If you have a bad time, suffer it, for you will have to go through all times, good and bad. He who tells people things to vex them will be told unpleasantries by them.

Be agreeable with people in the world. There is nothing more noble than the heart of man. He never receives subjection willingly. You will win more men through love than through force or fear. It is not courteous to say behind a man's back what you would be ashamed to say to his face.

My son, take note of four errors and guard against them; these are conceit, obstinacy, haste and sloth. The reward of conceit is abhorrence; the reward of obstinacy is dispute; the reward of haste is repentance; the reward of sloth is perdition. Since all extremes are evil, avoid them; for fear fears all things and daring dares to everything.

My son, serve the king and beware of him, for he is like a lion; he kills in play and destroys in jest. Beware of entering the king's house when his affairs are upset; for it will be a miracle if he who goes on the sea when it is disturbed will escape, and even more so if he goes on it when it is angry.

My son, fear not death in itself, for it is such a certainty that it cannot be avoided. We have come into the world under this condition, to be born and to die. Only he who has done much wrong and little good should fear death. Death is good for the good man because he goes to receive the reward for his goodness; it is good for the wicked because the earth may rest from his wickedness.

I do not wish to keep you longer, for now the time is approaching when you must show who you are, whence you came and where you hope to go."

So was this youth reared, and this good man taught and instructed him until he was fourteen years of age.

(Gutierre Díez de Games, *El Victorial,*
chapters 19 to 21)

A CHIVALRIC UNDERTAKING

If the passages from the *Victorial* tend to present an ideal of knighthood, the *Libro del paso honroso (Book of the Honorable Passage-at-arms)* shows what form that ideal could take in actual practice. This book is the record of real events that took place in the year 1434 and were written down by the scribe and notary public of the court, Pedro Rodríguez Delena, who witnessed all the ceremonies and incidents involved. The work has reached us in an abbreviated form from the sixteenth century. The subject matter is the month-long tourney that Suero de Quiñones and nine companions held against all knights who passed the bridge of Orbigo on the road to Santiago de Compostela, a heavily travelled thoroughfare. Suero de Quiñones was a member of an illustrious family, a poet of sorts and already famed for his prowess in arms. Of the sixty-eight challengers who took part in the tourney, four were foreigners; one knight each was from France, Italy, Germany and Portugal. The rest were Castilians, Aragonese and Catalans. One of the Castilian challengers was don Juan de Portugal, the son of Pero Niño (whose supposed education has just been presented) and his wife doña Beatriz.

The *Libro del paso honroso* is notable, not so much for its literary value or style —the repetition of episodes of the same kind becomes boring after a while— but as a document showing that life in the period was not far removed from the novels of chivalry. Suero de Quiñones' exploits seem like a quixotic show, before don Quixote, but they were not an isolated case. Jousts were one of the most common entertainments. This particular undertaking achieved a more widespread and permanent fame than others, and Cervantes recalled it over a hundred and seventy years later in his famous novel.

The selections that follow begin with the announcement of the tourney, six months prior to its inception, and the expensive and intensive preparations necessary for its success. The description of Suero and his companions as they came forth the first day, Sunday, July 11, 1434, reveals the stress placed on external show. It is also indicative of the strong French and Italian influences on courtly behaviour and dress.

Our most eminent and powerful King of Castile and Leon, don Juan II, was in the noble city of Medina del Campo with his wife, the very illustrious, virtuous and prudent lady doña María, his son and heir, the excellent Prince don Enrique, and the magnificent and famous lord, don Alvaro de Luna, his retainer, Grand Master of Santiago and Constable of Castile, and with many other illustrious prelates and knights of his magnificent court. On Friday, the first of January in the year of our Lord 1434, at approximately the first hour of evening, while he was attending great festivities and entertainments in his hall, there came before him with humble reverence the honorable knight Suero de Quiñones, with nine knightly companions, all very ingeniously armed in white; and expressing his respect through a herald named Vanguarda, he presented a petition couched in the following terms:

"It is just and reasonable for those who are in shackles and deprived of their freedom to desire liberty; and I, your vassal and subject, have been held enthralled by a lady for a long time now, as a sign of which I have worn around my neck every Thursday this iron chain, and this has been made known in your magnificent court and realms, and even beyond them, by the heralds who have worn similar fetters with my coat-of-arms. Now, most powerful lord, in the name of the Apostle St. James, I have arranged my ransom, which is that three hundred lances with Milanese tips are to be broken across the shaft by me and these knights here present in this armor, as will be detailed more fully in my articles of the joust, three lances being broken with every knight or gentleman who will come thereto, counting that blow which draws blood as a broken lance. This will take place this year, of which today is the first day, from two weeks preceding the day of St. James, mediator and patron of your subjects, to two weeks after, unless my ransom has been completed before that date. It will take place on the highway along which most people travel to the city which contains his holy tomb, and I assure all foreign knights and gentlemen who may come there that they will find equipment, horses, arms and lances such as any knight might dare to wield, without fearing that they will break from a slight blow. And let it be known to all ladies of honor that whosoever passes that place where I shall be, if she does not have a knight or gentleman to do battle for her, shall lose the glove from her right hand. But the above is understood with two exceptions, that neither your royal Majesty nor the magnificent Constable don Alvaro de Luna is to enter these trials."

After this petition was read by the aforementioned Vanguarda, the King went into council with his leading advisers, and finding that it should be conceded and granted, did so, according to the conditions set forth, so that the virtuous Suero de Quiñones might be freed from his bondage. Then the herald Vanguarda gave the proclamation in the hall where the King was, shouting aloud the following words: "Know all ye knights and gentlemen of our most noble lord, the King, that he does grant permission to this knight for this undertaking, observing the condition that neither the King, our lord, nor his Constable is to take part therein." After the proclamation was made, the honorable Suero de Quiñones approached one of the knights who were dancing in the hall, requesting that he help him remove his helmet. Then he mounted the steps of the dais where the King, Queen and Prince were seated and spoke the following: "Most powerful lord, I am indeed grateful to your lordship for having granted me this permission which I had resolved to ask of you, since it was so necessary to my honor, and I place my hope in God that in it I shall serve your royal Majesty as those from whom I am descended have served those powerful princes from whom your Majesty descends." Then he made obeisance to the King and Queen and withdrew with his honorable companions to disarm. Having done so, they donned suitable attire and returned to the hall to dance. When the dances were over, Suero de Quiñones had the rules of this undertaking read aloud.

Here the author gives the twenty-two articles governing the conditions for the actual tourney.

After the rules were read in the royal hall, the noble knight Suero de Quiñones, to explain and publicize his deed even more, gave a letter to Leon, king-at-arms of his majesty the King of Castile, the tenor of which was as follows: "You, Leon, king-at-arms, will make known to all the Kings, Dukes, Princes and lords to whose dominions you may come that I have been enthralled by a lady for a long time, and have concerted my ransom at three hundred lances, broken at the shaft, and that I cannot effect my release without the help of knights who will joust with me and my companions. You will offer my petitions that such knights will come to my aid, out of courtesy and love for their ladies, and you will, with the reverence due them, entreat those Kings, Dukes and Princes on my behalf, that the ladies of their realms be gracious and allow their knights and gentlemen to hasten to my deliverance. And so that the Kings, Dukes and Princes who are on a friendly footing with my lord, the noble King of Castile, will not be vexed that my enterprise is brought into their realms, you will inform their lordships how my lord, the King, seeing that my ransom cannot be accomplished without a goodly company of knights and gentlemen, has, on my behalf, granted his permission to all his subjects, among whom many are my close kindred. And if you should be further questioned by any knights and gentlemen concerning my undertaking or myself, you, king-at-arms, will be able to inform them of the permission and of all other things that I have made public in my rules of the joust, which I omit here to avoid vexatious prolixity."

After Leon, the king-at-arms, had received this letter from the hand of the virtuous knight Suero de Quiñones, signed with his name and sealed with his arms, and had received everything needed for the expenses of such a long journey, he promised to take it throughout the royal courts and have it publicly read, as was most suitable for it to attain its purpose. He also promised to have the same announcement made in other places by heralds whom he chose for that purpose. From the day on which permission to hold the tourney was granted until the time of the guarding of the passage was a period of five months, or a little more. During this time, the announcement was made in all of Christendom that could be reached. Also in this period, Suero de Quiñones set about seeking arms, horses and the other things necessary for such an important venture. While he was in Valladolid taking care of these arrangements, he sent men to cut much wood to make platforms, a jousting field and a hall. The master carpenters went to cut it in the forests of the districts of Luna, Ordas and Valdellamas, places which belong to the famous and noble knight, Diego Fernández de Quiñones, father of Suero de Quiñones, and which at the nearest point are five leagues distant from the Orbigo bridge. Many masters and laborers went forth for this task, with three hundred ox carts, according to the account of Pero Vivas de Laguna, the scribe appointed to receive the wood at the location of the Passage. Next to the highway to France there was a pleasant wooded field, in the middle of which the masters built a large wooden jousting field, one hundred and forty-six paces long and as much as a lance length high. In the middle of the lists they set up a row of boards, driven into the earth, some five and a half feet tall, and above them, another row of boards like a railing (in the way balconies are made), lengthwise of the course the horses would run. Around the lists they constructed seven platforms; one was at one end, near the gate to the lists through which Suero de Quiñones and his companions woud enter, so that they could watch the jousts when they themselves were not taking part. Further on were two other platforms, facing each other with the lists in between, from which could watch the foreign knights who might come to fight, both before and after doing so. Two other platforms were in the middle of the lists, facing each other. One was for the judges, the king-at-arms, messengers, trumpeters and scribes; and the other for the noble, famous and honored knights who might come to honor the Passage of Honor. The other two platforms were further on, for the people and the trumpeters and officers of the knights and gentlemen who came to the Passage. At each end of the lists was a gate; through one entered the defenders of the Passage, and there the arms of the Quiñones were placed on their flag, raised on high. Through the other entered the knights-errant who came to prove themselves at arms. There, too, was hoisted a flag with the coat-of-arms of Suero de Quiñones.

In addition to what has been told, a marble herald, the work of Nicolao Frances, master of the works at the church of Santa María de Regla in Leon, was constructed and set up on a marble base, finely adorned with clothing and a hat. Its left hand was at its side, and the right hand stretched out parallel to the highway to France and on it were letters saying: "This way to the Passage." This stone herald was placed on the highway to France some sixty paces beyond the bridge of San Marcos in the city of Leon. They finished putting it up, at considerable cost, on Saturday, the tenth of July, the first day of the jousts. On that same Saturday, twenty-two tents were erected in the field next to the Passage. Two of them were large and were placed near the gate to the lists through which entered the knights-errant, so that they could put on their armor in them. In the others both the knights-errant and the defenders, as well as the people who came to see the tourneys could lodge, together with all the necessary officers, such as kings-at-arms, heralds, trumpeters and other musicians, scribes, armorers, blacksmiths, surgeons, doctors, carpenters, lancemakers (to put the handles on the lances), tailors, embroiderers, etc. Futhermore, in the middle of the tents they made a well constructed hall, built of railings, thirty paces long and ten wide, all hung with rich French tapestries. In it were placed two tables, one for Suero de Quiñones and the knights who came to joust, and the other for the notable knights who came to see and honor the tourneys. At the front end of the hall was a large, rich sideboard, and near the hall ran one of the rivers that encompassed the field. Many great lords attended the festivities to do them honor, and Suero de Quiñones lodged them all honorably in places near the Passage that belonged to his father. Besides the nobles, there were many common people who gathered to enjoy such distinguished deeds of chivalry.

This same Saturday, two weeks before St. James' day, the king-at-arms, Portugal, and the herald, Monreal, informed the virtuous Suero de Quiñones at the gateway to the lists, in the presence of Pero Barba and Gómez Arias de Quiñones, the judges-elect, that there were three knights in the area of the Orbigo bridge, who were coming to the trials of the Honorable Passage. One was a German, named Micer Arnaldo de la Floresta Bermeja, from the Marquisate of Brandenburg in Upper Germany, a man of some twenty-seven years of age, blond and comely. The other two were Valencian brothers, of about the same age, whose names were Mosen Juan Fabla and Mosen Per Fabla, the sons of Mosen Juan Fabla, the lord of Chella. Suero de Quiñones was very pleased at the arrival of these knights, and more so when he learned that they seemed well versed in arms. He sent the herald and the king-at-arms to invite them to stay in his tent. They accepted and he received them very respectfully at the entrance to the lists, before the aforementioned judges. They said that, in accordance with his announcements sent through all Christendom, they had come to test themselves against him, and since this was the first of the days appointed for the jousts, they should begin at once, before the others came. Suero de Quiñones begged the two brothers not to force him to fight on Sunday, and also to give the first place in the jousting to the German knight, for he had been awaiting that day for two weeks. The two brothers granted him everything, even though first place was rightfully theirs because they had entered the lists before the German; but they yielded their right at his request and also said they would wait until Monday to joust. Then the judges, Pero Barba and Gómez Arias, notified the herald and the king-at-arms to remove the right spurs of the three knights, in accordance with the conditions made public concerning the guarding of the Honorable Passage, for they had entered fifty paces within the lists; they would be kept until the jousts were about to commence, when they would be restored to everyone. The spurs were removed and hung with solemn ceremony on a French tapestry on the judges' platform. The three knights paid homage to the judges and promised to remain until they tried their fortune, if the announced conditions were kept.

The next day, Sunday the eleventh of July, the trumpets and other musicians began to sound loudly at dawn, to arouse and move the hearts of the warriors to joust at arms. Suero de Quiñones and his nine companions arose and together heard mass in the Church of St. John, at the hospital maintained by the Order of St. John. Having returned to their lodging, they went forth soon after to receive the field and lists in the following manner: Suero de Quiñones came out on a powerful steed, with blue caparisons embroidered with the emblem and iron chain of his famous undertaking, and above each emblem were letters saying: "Il faut delibrer." He wore a quilted doublet of olive cut-velvet with green brocade, and an outer tunic of blue cut-velvet with olive brocade. He had scarlet Italian breeches, a tall pointed scarlet cap and richly ornamented Italian spurs. In his hand he held a bare golden sword. He wore on his right upper arm his emblem richly worked in gold, some two fingers wide, with blue letters around it which said:

> Si a vous ne plaist de ouyr mesure
> Certes je dy
> Que je suy
> Sans venture.

There were, furthermore, small round gold ornaments around the emblem. He wore his leg armor and bracers with handsome gracefulness. Behind him went three pages on beautiful horses, their blue doublets and surcoats with the famous emblem, and all dressed as we have said above. The caparisons of the first page's horse were of red damask with a sable border, embroidered with thick silver rounds like the small plates on a helmet. On his head he wore a helmet, above which was represented a large golden tree with green leaves and golden apples, and from the foot of it coiled a green snake. It was similar to the tree at which Adam is depicted as having sinned. In the middle of the tree was a bare sword with letters saying: "Le vrai ami." This page carried his lance in his hand. The second page was wearing a quilted doublet and scarlet breeches like the first, his lance in his hand, and with caparisons of olive cut-velvet with blue brocade. The third page was dressed in the same manner as the other two and the trappings of his horse were of crimson cut-velvet with rich edgings and adornments that made it very beautiful.

In front of Suero de Quiñones rode the nine companions of his enterprise, one after the other, dressed in their doublets and scarlet Italian breeches, with tall scarlet caps and their blue tunics embroidered with the handsome emblem and iron chain of their captain, Suero, and with their leg armor and bracers pleasingly alike. The caparisons of their horses were blue, embroidered with the same emblem and above each emblem were embroidered letters saying: "le faut delibrer." In front of these nine knights were led two large, fine horses, pulling a cart filled with lances with strong Milanese tips. These were of three kinds; some very stout, some medium and others thin, although capable of delivering a moderate blow. Over the lances were some blue and green trappings embroidered with rosebays in bloom, and on each tree was the figure of a parrot. Above it all sat a dwarf who drove the cart. In front of everything else went the trumpeters of the King and of the knights, with Moorish drums and flutes which had been brought there by the judge Pero Barba...

> As previously noted, the detailed account of the 727 clashes between defenders and challengers becomes somewhat tedious. One of the more interesting encounters is that of Lope de Estúñiga and a certain Francés Davío, not because it differs essentially from the others, but because of Davíos' reason for taking part and the author's scandalized reaction.

The following Friday, the sixteenth of July, after reveille was played by the trumpeters and morning mass was heard (as was the custom of those guarding the Honorable Passage), there entered the lists in good knightly order Lope de Estúñiga, as defender, wearing over his armor a half tunic, one side of blue cut-velvet brocade and the other side of green and white damask, and Mosen Francés Davío, as challenger. In the first charge, Mosen struck Estúñiga on the left wrist guard and, breaking off the tip of his lance, left it stuck there. Estúñiga's lance struck his opponent's lance shaft near the tip, took off a splinter and travelled its length until it hit the shaft guard, where it left a good mark; from this encounter all of his lance rest was stripped and its bridges broken, and his neck guards and gauntlet were unfastened, so that he had to disarm; and neither of them broke a lance. After Estúñiga's armor was replaced, they ran three more charges without an encounter, but in the fifth, Mosen struck Estúñiga's shaft guard and, glancing off it, hit his brassard and unhitched it, piercing it with the tip of his lance and breaking his lance staff. They ran seven more times without meeting, although in one they crossed. At the thirteenth charge, Estúñiga struck Mosen's left wrist guard, without either breaking his lance or having any misadventure. They carried out three more in which they did not connect but at the seventeenth, Estúñiga struck Mosen's left brassard without piercing it, but he broke his lance on it. Then they ran five more times with no encounter, although in one Estúñiga grazed his opponent's armor with his lance. At the twenty-third charge, Estúñiga struck Mosen on the left wrist guard and inflicted a good mark without piercing it, and he broke off its joint pin, knocking it to earth; and he broke his lance in pieces. The tip and a piece of the shaft flew high into the air, over the judges' platform, and fell more that four feet outside the lists. With this they had completed their joust and the judges sent them off in peace. Mosen Francés declared in the presence of many knights who heard him that he swore to God never again to have anything to do with a nun or to love one, because he had loved one until this time and it was to please her that he had come to this joust; and he said that anyone who heard that he loved a nun could challenge him as a dissolute fellow, without his being able to reply at all. To this I say that if he had had any Christian nobility, or even the natural shame with which all men try to cover their faults, he would not have publicized such a scandalous sacrilege, so dishonorable to convent life and so injurious to Jesus Christ. Mosen was taken to his lodging with a great company of knights on foot and horseback, and with a loud fanfare of music, after thanking Estúñiga for having jousted with him; and they remained good friends. Estúñiga was accompanied from the lists with very honorable pomp.

The following short passage presents a little side event to the main purpose of proving military skill and valor.

After Negrete and Suero had concluded their joust, there came to the Honorable Passage that same afternoon a trumpeter from Lombardy, who had travelled on a pilgrimage to Santiago in Galicia. While he was there he heard that at the Passage by the Orbigo bridge was a trumpeter of the King of Castile, named Dalmao, who was very famous for his skill, and he had gone thirty leagues out of his way to challenge him at music. Of two very fine trumpets that he brought, he put up one against one of Dalmao's. The latter, taking this trumpet of the Lombard's, played it with such vigor and such a variety of tunes and harmonies that the Lombard, after he did everything he knew how, acknowledged defeat and gave him his trumpet, which Dalmao accepted and immediately returned. He invited him to be his guest all the time he wished to stay there, and the Lombard became his very good friend.

> The encounter between Suero de Quiñones and the Aragonese Esberte de Claramonte reminds us that jousts of this kind were essentially war games and, as such, held a considerable element of danger for the participants. Because the Church disapproved of tourneys, they risked not only life and limb, but also their immortal souls.

On Friday morning, the sixth of August, Mosen Francés Pero Baste, an Aragonese of the household of Mosen Juan de Bardaxi, entered the field, presented himself to the judges to try his fortune, and after the usual solemnities were carried out, was admitted to the trials. Then Suero, son of Alvar Gómez de Quiñones, [1] entered the lists as defender, although he was not yet recovered from the wound we previously wrote that he had received; and as challenger came the unfortunate Esberte de Claramonte, an Aragonese. They ran the first charge without meeting, but in the second, the Aragonese struck Suero on the guard of his lance, rebounded to his right brassard and disarmed it, without breaking his lance; and neither suffered any misadventure. After this they made four more charges without an encounter. The Aragonese was riding a horse that shied at the moment of impact and for that reason he asked

---

[1] Previously, the name of Suero's father was given as Diego Fernández de Quiñones. One of his nine companions was Alvaro, son of Alvar Gómez de Quiñones.

for the horse that his opponent, Suero, was riding, as it seemed better trained to him. Suero gave it to him out of courtesy and because it was one of the rules of the guarding of the Honorable Passage. But he who sought such improvements was far from equally seeking out greater dangers to gain greater honor, which was the purpose of this venture. When both were back on horseback, they made the seventh charge, and Suero struck the Aragonese over the visor of his helmet. His lance bent, without breaking, and neither had any misadventure. At the eighth charge, Suero again hit the Aragonese on the left brassard and unharnessed it, leaving the point of his lance in it ; the lance tip expanded from the force of the impact and broke his lance to pieces, but neither suffered misadventure. At the ninth and sad charge, Suero again hit the unhappy knight Claramonte and struck the visor of his helmet, running the whole tip of his lance through his left eye and into his brain, and knocking his eye out of his head. He broke his lance a span from the tip. Claramonte lowered his lance so much that it hit the ground and the tip stuck there and broke. Impelled both by the blow given and the blow received, he was knocked back out of the saddle onto the rump of his horse and reached the end of the lists, where he fell to the ground and died at once, without uttering a word. When they removed his helmet, they found his right eye was swollen as big as a fist and his face had the look of a man dead for two hours.

All the Aragonese and Catalans present lamented greatly for the unfortunate victim, and Suero, who had killed him, wept more bitterly than all the rest, being truly grieved at such a misfortune. Suero de Quiñones provided all possible honors for the body, nor did he forget the man's soul. He sent for his confessor, Friar Antonio, and for the other monks he had there, to administer the sacraments, and he begged him to sing a responsory over the body, as is the custom of Holy Church, as if he himself were the victim. The friar told him that Holy Church does not consider those who die in such exercises as its children, for they cannot be considered to be without mortal sin, nor does it pray to God for them, but leaves them condemned to eternal punishment, as Canon Law commands, in the title on tourneys. But at Suero's request he took a letter to the Bishop of Astorga, entreating him to grant permission to bury the victim in holy ground, and Suero promised, if the permission were granted, to take the body to Leon and give it burial in the Quiñones' family chapel in the church of St. Isidore. In the meanwhile, they took the body to a hermitage of St. Catherine's which is at the end of the Orbigo bridge, as one is going from Astorga to Leon, and it remained there until nightfall, when the friar returned without the permission. And so they buried him outside of hallowed ground, near that hermitage, with the greatest honor they could and with many tears shed by the knights who attended.

> At the end of the designated period of time, only a hundred and sixty-six lances, of the three hundred vowed, had been broken, but the judges declared themselves satisfied and freed Suero de Quiñones of his oath. They also granted each knight who had taken part a certificate of participation.

The honorable judges, Pero Barba and Gómez de Quiñones, were pleased to comply with the request of the valorous Lope de Estúñiga, and ordered the scribes who had been present at the deeds of arms to present to each and every one a signed affidavit which would, in any place and before any people, attest what that person had done for his everlasting honor in the exercise of arms at the defense of the Honorable Passage.

> (Pedro Rodríguez Delena, *Libro del paso honroso,* chapters 3-5, 7-12, 25, 59, 63, 76.)

DAILY LIFE

FOOD AND SERVICE

One of the most interesting books for the customs of our period is the *Arte Cisoria, o tratado del arte de cortar del cuchillo* (*Treatise on the Art of Carving*), by Enrique de Aragón, known also as Enrique de Villena, whose *Doze Trabajos de Hércules* we utilized previously for the classes of society.

Enrique de Aragón (1384-1434) was one of the most bizarre figures to appear in Spanish letters and he has gone down in history as a grotesque misfit. He was descended from the royal houses of Castile and Aragon, being the son of don Pedro of Aragon and doña Juana, a natural daughter of Enrique II of Castile. His cousin and protector was the much admired don Fernando de Antequera, regent of Castile and later King of Aragon. Enrique de Aragón's life was a series of mis-steps; he failed in his attempts to gain the title of Marquis of Villena, which had originally been granted to his grandfather; he had his marriage annulled, alleging impotency, in order to qualify for the post of Grand Master of the Order of Calatrava, and not only failed to get that post, but also lost other honors he had relinquished in exchange for it (the annulment of his marriage was also set aside by the Pope). Pérez de Guzmán, who included a portrait of him in his *Generaciones y semblanzas,* wrote that Enrique de Aragón was "indifferent and remote, not only to chivalry, but even to the business of the world, and in the governing of his house and estate he was so incompetent and inept that it was most surprising." Although Villena was admired for his learning by such enlightened contemporaries as Juan de Mena and the Marquis of Santillana, he had a reputation, even during his lifetime, for being a sorcerer and in league with the devil (he was interested in the occult sciences and in fortune telling), and at his death his library was ordered burned by Juan II. His known works include, besides those already named, a *Tractado del aojamiento o fascinología (Treatise on the evil-eye)*, indicative of his interest in the occult, and an *Arte de Trovar (Art of composing poetry)*. The latter work, unfortunately incomplete, is an adaptation of the poetics of the Provençal troubadors. The most engaging portions of it describe the poetic tournaments held in Zaragoza and Barcelona under the direction of the author, when Fernando de Antequera became King of Aragon. Villena deserves credit also for his translations. At the behest of Juan II of Navarre, he made the first complete version of the *Aeneid* in a modern language, and for the Marquis of Santillana he translated Dante's *Divine Comedy*.

The *Arte cisoria,* from which the following excerpts on food are taken, was written for the royal carver, Sancho de Járava. After a brief and inventive history of the art of carving, the author treats the conditions and customs necessary for the person holding this position, describes the different implements he uses, and then tells of various foods and how they are prepared and served. These are presented in four chapters: edible birds, four-footed animals, fish, and fruits and vegetables. The final chapters of the book discuss the honors due the carver, punishment for failure in office, various ranks of servants and their training. Stylistically the work suffers from obscurity, because of the author's attempt to Latinize his language, especially through the use of hyperbaton.

On the qualities and customs that pertain to the carver, especially before a king.

It is reasonable that the person who is to serve in the office of carver before any lord, and especially before a king, should have good habits, for, just as the king's dignity is preeminent, so should his servants be most painstaking in tastes and manners, especially he who is to carve before him, for the king sees him in front of him every day, so close that only the table separates them; and although he may have every good custom in general, because of the special nature of that service to which he is appointed, he should, above all else, be loyal in guarding the king's health and life, so that when he is cutting the food (or at any other time), he should not put, nor consent to be put on it anything that might bring death, disease or other harm to him, attending to this with all his strength and power. He should be persuaded to such loyalty by fear of the king, zeal for goodness, fear of shame from the people, love of the king he serves and consideration for his reputation, which would be sullied after his death, to say nothing of the legal punishment he would suffer; and above all else he should be free of greed, which more than anything makes men err in this. The second requirement is cleanliness; he should always keep himself well groomed, according to his station, with his beard shaven, his hair cut, his nails frequently trimmed and his face and hands carefully washed, so that nothing unbecoming appears in him. He should avoid wearing boots, especially new ones, and lining that smells bad from the dressing; his nails should be trimmed moderately, but not too close, and cleaned every morning; and his hand should be adorned with rings that have stones or settings that are efficacious against poison and corrupt air, such as the ruby, diamond, zircon, emerald, unicorn's horn, serpentine, bezoar, and other counterpoisons, such as that made from the heart of a man killed by poisoning and burned, or rather hardened and petrified, in a reverberatory furnace. Alexander always carried this with him, above all others, as Aristotle tells in his Lapidary. He should also protect his hands with clean and sweet smelling gloves, except when he is carving or eating. These gloves should not be lined with fur, because the fur might stick to the hands, and some furs, such as that of the fox or cat, are unhealthy; but they should be made of worn buckskin and scarlet cloth, sewn by needle. In his eating and drinking, so that he will not belch, spit, cough, yawn, sneeze or have bad breath, he should preferably use sauces, linaloa, mastic, citron rind, lemon leaves and rosemary blossoms, which make the breath sweet and healthy. He should keep his teeth clean and scoured with those things that penetrate to the gums and keep them clean, such as ground coral and resin, calcined alum, cloves and cinnamon, all mixed with ground pumice and prepared with skimmed honey; and cleanse them of the tartar, if there is any, removing each day after every meal the food lodged there, with a gold pick, doing so without pressure, but gently, so as not to cause any lesion to the gums or draw blood from them; and then rub them with scarlet cloth.

In the third place he should be quiet, so that when he is carving he does not talk, or make disagreeable or unmannered faces, or be looking at someone else; but he should only watch the king, with humility, and what he is carving. Neither should he scratch his head or anywhere else, or blow his nose, so that the king will not see in him anything of bad appearance, at which he might be disgusted or angered. In the fourth place, he should be skilled in the diligence and promptness required of his position, with his mind on his work and free of other considerations, so he will not commit any fault through inattention; he should fix his eyes on the food, after it is brought to the table and given into his care, so that no one can approach it or throw anything suspicious on it, watching always for when he is ordered to carve and when to leave off. Before and after serving he should wash his hands studiously, and he should carefully look to see if any different colors appear on the food that do not belong to such a dish, or if it has any odor or bad taste, and he should not cut from that piece. In addition, he should refrain from the things contrary to the qualities and habits set forth above, especially from eating garlic, onions, leeks, coriander, scallions, and the electuary made from the leaf of the hemp, which the Moors call hashhish, for such things cause bad breath. He should keep away from large fires in hearths and from smoky kitchens, ovens, the fumes from cauldrons, and places where they smelt metals, so that odors from the fumes will not stick to his clothes. He should keep away from stables, slaughterhouses, sewers, tanneries, places where furs are dressed, or where they make vermilion, glass, soap, or scrape parchments, and any such places where odors might cling to him and infect his clothing, and from which he might carry away filth on his feet. Let him beware the excess use of women, for the bodies of such men stink, especially if they do it right after they have eaten or when they are dressed, for the food becomes corrupted and furnishes a fetid nutriment to the limbs, and clothing takes on the corrupt odor and retains it. For that reason Aristotle said in his proem that dogs serve such men, because of that stench that they smell. Also, he should not carry in his hands anything that smells bad, such as asarabacca, or *flores de santo,* rose wood, boxwood, asafoetida or fenugreek or the like. He should not eat hot foods or drink hot broths or other liquids that harm the teeth very much and give them a bad appearance. Finally, avoid all things that are contrary to cleanliness and good fragrance...

*In what manner the office of carver should be served and
carried out with care.*

He who has such a position, of caring for the royal eating,
should be careful and solicitous, especially at meal time, so he does
not have to be waited for, called and received angrily, for he
is appointed to a position of care and trust in which special training is required to be conducted in an orderly and uniform manner,
as befits a skilled and learned calling. Hence, when he sees that
the king is about to sit down at the table, he should go to the place
where the butlers keep the plate ready; then, having brought out
that small chest of his that we have talked about, he should open it
and place on a silver basin the cloths for cleaning the knives, of
somewhat coarser linen, so the roughness will better remove any
refuse from the knife; and there should be two or three, so there
will be enough if the meal is prolonged and he will not have to
ask for such a cloth while he is at his task of carving, especially if
the sauces and dressings are many. On these, place the thin napkins
for wiping the king's mouth and hands while he is eating; there
should be a half dozen, so when one has served he can be given
another, before the smears from wiping on it become apparent, and
even though they are not all used each day, it is foresight and good
appearance and there might come a time when they are needed;
therefore it is better to have a sufficient supply of such cloths.
Above these place the five carving knives, previously described, and
the other instruments I named in the preceding chapter; above
it all place a thin, embroidered cloth to cover it, and leave it like
this in the care of the butler, who should be a trustworthy person.

When the king is seated and is washing his hands, after the
bread has been served and the blessing said, the carver should have
a butler bring before him that basin he has prepared with the napkins and instruments; he should go with it to the table and, kneel-
ing, he takes the basin and puts it on the table, to the right of
where he is to serve. He removes the cloth and spreads it out on
the table at one end, toward himself, and on it places the knives in
order, with those used first and needed most nearest him. He should
have handy a rush basket, covered on the outside with red embossed
leather and lined inside with linen; it should be near him, under the
table, where he can put the napkins when they are soiled, so they

will not be seen after they are stained, while the clean ones remain in the basin. This basket should be brought in and placed under the table by a trustworthy man of the carver's.

After the carver has laid out his knives, as described, he should immediately test the knives before him and the other instruments in the basin, making little slices with each of the knives and instruments, passing each through each slice, through the areas that will touch the food, and these slices should be eaten by the butler who was entrusted to bring in the basin. This test could be made with a single slice, passing all the instruments through it, but it is better for each knife to make its own slice. In some places it is customary for the carver to test the salt, and this is all right when the salt cellar is brought in with the knives, but it is better for it to be brought alone and for the carver to take care of and test only his own instruments.

While this is being done, the food arrives. Then he should arise and withdraw from the table, so the steward or chief waiter and taster can have room to place the food and make his tests, as is the custom, but he should always keep his eye on his knives and basin and anyone who approaches them, so he can give an accounting to the person in charge. After the steward has withdrawn, the carver should return to his position and place one of the napkins in the basin before the king, first bringing it up to his mouth as a test... Then he uncovers the food and carves from the part that is best or that he knows will please the king most, or that he asks for, as I shall describe in the following chapters on carving food, placing the food he wishes to carve on another flat platter, leaving the rest covered, as it was. He should clean the knives with which he is cutting often, before any food or fat sticks to them, and avoiding as much as possible touching the food with his hands, but holding it with the three-pronged forks [1] I have described.

He should have nearby another small basin in which to throw the parings and bones and left-overs from what he has carved, so that he does not put them back on the trays where the food is. Some people are wont to throw this in the vessel or basin where the king throws bones, but it is better to have another one, so the king

---

[1] These were carving tools; forks for eating, as we know them, were not used.

does not see the torn up food right before him and will not be offended by a mass of bones, which might disgust him when he puts his left-overs there; but he can put there a few crumbs or pieces of bread that are left on the table, taking them up with the fourth knife, which is best for this, before he places food before the king.

The carver must make a test of everything he cuts by eating a little of it; then he places, with the end of the knife, the carved food on the plate from which the king eats. On it he will neatly put salt with the knife, smoothing it with the point, if the food should be eaten with salt, having made the test thereof by taking some with a little bread and eating it. If the food that is to be served does not fit on the knife, transfer it with a fork or knife to another platter and serve it from that; be careful not to put much food at a time on the platter, to avoid satiety, but wait until it is necessary to add more, so the king may eat at his leisure, neatly and cleanly, and without complaint.

Bread should be served by placing it before him with the two-tined fork, if it is freshly baked; and if it is hard, by slicing it with the carving knife and placing it on a tray within reach, so he can take it when he will. So that the food can be kept warmer, the carver should have ready on the platter where he carves a loaf of bread, smooth on both sides and as thick as a hand, hard and rolled out with a pin, so it does not have eyes or airholes. This loaf should be brought to the table with the rest of the bread by the girl who serves the bread. He should use the carving knife to make thin slices the length of the loaf, so they do not fold over, and, placing them on the platter, carve more neatly, while keeping the food from cooling off so quickly; he carves and places it before the king, transferring it to the king's plate with a fork.

The same service applies to meat, bowls of soup, sauces, the adding of ground spices where they are needed, sugar, vinegar or honey, as the foods require, and pomegranate, orange or lemon juice, etc., always tasting them first. This should all be done quickly, so the king does not have to ask or wait for it, nor should the carver have to be reminded of it by anyone.

When the king takes wine, remove the plate from which he is eating from in front of him, so wine or water does not fall on it; keep it on one side before him, raised on high, while making room for the cupbearer to fulfill his office. When that is done, place the plate before him again, if the food is still good and hot; if not, give him a new plate.

Use a different plate each time a new dish is served, so it can be served neatly and so the flavors of different foods do not mix, and so people present will not think there is any lack or poverty of table service. When the plates are changed, clean the tablecloth in front of the king with a napkin, if any food or bread has fallen on it, or pick it up with the broad knife and put it in the vessel where the king throws bones. When the carver is not cutting, he should watch the king, and if there is any food on his face or chest, make him a secret sign to remove it, so he will always appear neat and clean.

While carving, he should take care not to breathe on the table, or have his arms sticking out, but use only his hands and present a sober and elegant appearance, arranging and displaying those implements he expects or knows will be necessary to serve with. And if the king is eating privately, because he has been out hunting, and all these things cannot be done as fully as indicated, do those that time and means allow, preserving those most necessary to maintain cleanliness.

The carver should take care not to turn his head elsewhere while he is serving, unless he is called for some necessary purpose; nor should he look anywhere else, but be intent on what he is to do, giving all his attention to it.

When he has finished serving, he should return the wiped-off knives and instruments to the basin in which they came, and cover them with the embroidered cloth that he spread out, on which they rested on the table; then he gives them to the butler who brought them, who is waiting there, and returns with him to the place where the table service is kept. There he has them washed better, puts them in their racks and places them in the aforementiond chest. The man who brought it from his rooms, or the lieutenant entrusted to this by the carver, should carry it before him. A youth should take out the basket in which the soiled napkins were placed, to take care of having them cleaned and keep account of them. Although it was not mentioned before that this basket should be brought in with the chest, it should be understood; since it is designated to receive the napkins, it should be brought in when the chest comes in, by that youth who takes it out. The carver should keep these things in a safe and secure place in his room, so that no one can get to them, except by his order and consent. If any of the knives or instruments becomes jagged, broken or twisted, he should have it repaired by a trustworthy person. It would be a good idea, for this, to have skilled knife makers and silver smiths, known persons and natives of the realm, follow the court and be appointed exclusively for this work, leaving other tasks aside, and they ought to be given a suitable wage, so they would not be the losers by devoting themselves solely to this.

On the carving of edible birds.

...Let us commence, then, with the peacock, which is customarily eaten roasted, and sometimes on festive occasions, with its tail still attached, it being wrapped in damp cloths [*while roasting*] to preserve it and keep it from scorching. The same thing is done with the neck, although a better method is to remove the tail and neck, and when the fowl is roasted fasten them back with wooden sticks, so they do not impart any undesirable flavor to the meat. The tail is opened in a fan and around the neck is placed a kind of little mantilla of gold cloth or heavy silk on which is painted the king's coat-of-arms. The body of the peacock is larded with strips of seasoned bacon about as wide as one's hand, which cover it completely and are tied on with red silk threads, or any other threads, which gives it a good flavor. If it is brought like this, carve in the following manner:

Having removed the neck and tail, proceed to the carving; and if they are not brought in, one begins in the same way, first removing the wrapping of bacon, having cut the threads. Although few people eat it, it is put on so that the fat will penetrate the bird and keep the juices from running out, for if they did, it would be very dry and less tasty. When this is removed, the peacock is ready; first of all the carver should remove the feet with the fourth knife, previously mentioned, take off the wing tips, and throw them and the feet in the basin in which I said he should put the bones. Then he cuts one wing and removes it from the side with the same knife, and makes incisions in the meat, a little apart, but with some touching, so that when it is eaten it is not necessary to pull very much; in that state he puts it on a small plate and from there transfers it to the plate from which the king eats. While he is eating that, carve the leg on the same side, removing it whole from the peacock. Cleave it in two parts at the joint, remove the entire skin from the leg, setting it aside; holding the thigh bone with the three-tined fork, use the second knife to cut thick slices of that meat, each a mouthful, until little is left on the bone. After this, cut up the skin in small pieces, mix it with those slices, because it is better to eat it together with the meat, and place it all on the plate, waiting until he has eaten a little of that. When he has nearly finished, or does not seem to want any more, the bones are thrown in the aforementioned basin, for it is not suitable that they be gnawed at the royal dinner. Then proceed to carve the breast on the side from which the leg was removed, making a cut over it lengthwise, so it passes near the shoulder, and running the knife through, and from that remove cross slices as wide and long as possible, but suitably thin, as I indicated when I told how to cut with the first knife, placing each one on the eating plate with the knife, thus using up the breast meat nearly to the middle of the breast bone. Then turn the bird sideways, holding the wing with the left hand, and, raising it up, make a cross cut under the bottom to open and lift out the meat, and make thin slices and place them with the knife, like the first slices, until the meat is gone there. Then make another cut over the back part, making thin slices until it is used up, as has been described for carving the wing... When one side is completely carved, the other side is done in the same way.

Then, over the flat part of the croup, where it is fat, carve off thin slices until the bone shows; next, the back part can be broken... Afterwards, remove the breast and cleave it in two parts with the point of the second knife, striking the back of the knife with your hand. In the same way and with the same knife are made the two openings I mentioned, from the rear, and the middle of the breastbone can be easily removed and divided into two parts, and additional pieces can be made from the croup and spine, but this should be omitted in the presence of the king, unless he especially asks for it. The carving done before this should be enough to furnish sufficient food that can be eaten neatly, without gnawing bones or holding in the hand large bones that have to be bitten into many times; but if he asks for it, the carving and slicing of those parts should be done with the third knife. Thus the peacock will be completely carved, neatly and skillfully, and with the proficiency it deserves, according to the different parts, and considering the people for whom it is carved. These slices should be made, because it is a large bird and they can be chewed more easily, but they must be wide enough so they can be found in the mouth and the pleasure of their taste can better be enjoyed. And so that it can be carved more quickly, before it gets cold, slice off only the meat that can be gotten at neatly, dividing the remainder and the bones from which the little meat left on could not readily be removed, for other people of lesser rank.

Large and heavy birds, such as crane, goose, duck, pheasant, francolin, widgeon, rooster, capon, heron, wild duck, white duck and the like, should be carved in the same manner, except that with the capon, rooster and widgeon the breast-bone and the croup are not broken into two parts, and geese, cranes, herons and wild ducks are not brought to the table with the feet attached.

Hens are carved in the same way, except that the incision under the wing is not made, nor those over the croup, nor that in the leg, except to separate it in two pieces, but they make some long slices in it, and do not divide the breast-bone or croup, because they are small as compared with the other, bigger fowl. Thus they can be served whole, except that on the rear part, they make some slices toward the bone so that there, where there is more flesh, it can be removed with less trouble. They divide the spine in two pieces, taking out the croup in the skin, lengthwise, as much as possible. The same applies to the eggs, if it has any; placed on a fork and trimmed of their membrane, they are served whole, with the ovary; but in the presence of the king one should not worry much about serving the lungs that are left in it, or the testicles of roosters and such trifles that are deemed delicacies, but give little sustenance, unless they are requested...

Partridges are served in another manner when they are roasted. When they are brought in whole, remove the feet and wings and put them on the eating plate; because they are small pieces, chewing on them is not disturbing, and they are tasty and increase the appetite. The wing tips are removed unless someone asks for them. This is done with the fourth knife. Then open the leg with the second knife, without cutting completely through, put salt in the cut and cover it over again as it originally was. Next, open the wing; starting at the shoulder and holding the end of the wing, pull firmly, using the knife, until the wing is almost separated from that side of the body. Put salt in the opening, as for the leg, cover it again and press it back. Gently turn it over, so as not to separate the wing and leg that were cut, and do the same thing on the other side. Afterwards, open the breast-bone part, without cutting all the way through, and salt it; then make two cuts on either side of the croup, which go in as far as the bone, and give it a blow on the backbone with the cutting edge of the knife, so it cracks it in half without cutting through. Let it stand a while until the salt melts and penetrates the meat to give it flavor. Then sprinkle on lemon juice, which is the most suitable of the sour flavors, tempered with rose water to moderate its sharpness, if it is spring or summer; and if it is autumn or cold weather, it is better to use orange juice with a little chicken broth to temper it; if this is not available, use the juice of bittersweet pomegranates or plain water, because these things alone make it tender and give it flavor. If the person for whom you are carving likes it, place thin slices of bread underneath, for they are agreeable to eat with the partridge, soaked in this juice. In very cold weather, put salt, pepper and white wine in the cuts, instead of the juices. Some people serve it whole, cut like this, to the person who is to eat it, but it is a more genteel and neater service to serve the legs, wings, wishbone, breastbone and the part from the middle back, with the croup, as separate pieces, leaving the rest in the basin for bones. This is more desirable before the king and noble people who eat neatly and delicately...

(Enrique de Villena, *Arte cisoria,* chapters 3, 5, 7.)

CLOTHING AND COSMETICS

Considerable detail concerning masculine attire can be found in historical accounts (see above, the description of the battle of Olmedo from the *Crónica de don Álvaro de Luna,* or the presentation of knights coming forth to joust in the *Paso honroso* held by Suero de Quiñones), but women's accoutrements are neglected in such works. This oversight is very well remedied by the work of a fifteenth century moralist, Alonso Martínez de Toledo, Archpriest of Talavera (1398 - c. 1470). A royal chaplain, Martínez de Toledo composed several works of an erudite character on history and hagiography, but his enduring fame rests almost entirely on a little book that he himself left untitled, saying, "unbaptized, let it be called by name the Archpriest of Talavera wherever it may be taken." Posterity has usually given it the title of *Corbacho o reprobación del amor mundano (The Lash, or reprobation of worldly love),* most probably because of a vague resemblance in subject matter to Boccaccio's *Il Corvaccio,* although the tone and purpose of the two works are quite dissimilar.

The *Corbacho* is divided into four parts: the first is an attack on worldly love, the second treats of the ways and wiles of women, the third deals with the temperaments of men and the influence on them of the planets, and the fourth is a condemnation of beliefs in fate, fortune telling and the like. As a satiric painter of customs, Talavera has no equal in his period. He was a cultured humanist, but the sources for his best writing were from life, from stories he heard or things he saw. He attacks vice, but he knows about it from experience and reveals a certain delectation in cataloguing the seamier aspects of life. One cannot really consider him a misogynist, because he is too fascinated by the foibles of women to really hate them. He is much more interesting (and interested) when he is writing about them than when he considers men, and for this reason the last two parts of his book are generally considered inferior to the first two. Stylistically the *Corbacho* might be said to suffer from schizofrenia: on the one hand the author employs a rather stilted, elegant manner of writing predominant in his time; on the other, he piles up examples of popular speech in veritable outbursts of exuberance.

The passages presented here are all from the second section of the *Corbacho,* wherein Talavera claims he will applaud virtuous women as well as expose the vices of the wicked. His emphasis, however, is entirely on the latter. The first selection paints, through the agency of an envious gossip, a picture of a girl in her Easter finery; the second lays bare the clothing, adornment and cosmetics that females hoard away in their chests; and the final passage gives the preparations and behaviour of a woman going on an outing.

That woman is a gossip and a slanderer is a general rule: for if she talks with a thousand, she talks about a thousand: how they walk, how they feel, what their status in life is, how they live, how they act. To be silent is death for her. She could not spend a single hour without defaming both the good and the bad. No man or woman strikes her as good, either in the town square or in church, as she says: "Oh, how dolled-up Whats-her-name was Easter Sunday. A fine scarlet dress with marten lining, a Florentine skirt edged in fur trimming, a hand-span wide, her brocade-lined train dragging ten spans behind her, a sable-lined cloak with its collar half way down her back, brocaded sleeves, gold rosary beads, of twelve to the ounce, a bracelet of pearls, which were a quarter carat in size, gold pendant earrings that covered her whole neck, a hairnet edged with white lilies worked with so much silver that they dazzled me, a rich bodkin that is the height of elegance, of fine gold thread with a lot of pearl work, her chignon covered with gold ornaments and of cambric drawn-work, all trimmed with fig leaves of silver embroidery hung with crescents, pendants and circles, with rich lace trimming. Besides, a veil with which she covered her face, so she looked like the Queen of Sheba, to show off her beauty. Moorish bracelets of amber set in gold, ten or twelve rings, among which are two diamonds, a saphire, two emeralds; marten-lined gloves to shine her face and adjust her make-up. She was shining like a sword with her cosmetics; a silk girdle with gold bosses, the end carefully done with a moonshaped clasp very prettily worked; painted and brocade clogs nearly a span high; six women accompanying her, a girl to carry her train, a perfumed peacock whisk; and she was perfumed and scented, her brows made fragrant with civet, and shining like a sword..."

It would be a great sin to doubt that woman is a grasper and usurper to right and left, inasmuch as she will fearlessly and shamelessly take as much as she can snatch or pilfer, not only from strangers and those unknown to her, but even from her relatives and friends. It is not in her nature to give, and so it befalls a man with a woman as with a father and mother with their child: let the father or mother give their son everything he desires and never say no to him; then let them take from him a little crust of bread or anything else he may be holding; he cries and shouts for it, even though they gave it to him in the first place. Or let the father or mother say to their son, to test him: "Son, give me this, for I am your father." Then he flees with it and turns his face. So is it with a woman: give to her and she will take, singing; ask her for something and she will weep and grumble. And what they take and steal in that manner they hide in chests and coffers or tied up in rags, so they look like shop keepers or haberdashers, and when they begin to lay open their chests, there they have pearls, there rings, here earrings, there bracelets, many wimples trimmed with silk and veiling, gauze hair coverings, three or four *lenzarejas*,[1] many different kinds of cambrics, Catalan coifs, crests with silver embroidery, embroidered arm bands, hair nets, bodkins, ribbons, coifs, belts, skirt trains, bracelets of pearls and of black beads, or others, with blue stones, ten thousand to a bracelet, of different designs, ornamented ruffs of wimple silk or thin linen, blouse sleeves of wimple material fit for a trousseau, embroidered chemises (there is no equal to this!), shirred or unshirred sleeves, others embroidered or ready to be embroidered, handkerchiefs by the dozen, and more purses and richly worked gold and silver belts, brooches, a mirror, cosmetic jar, a comb and sponge with gum for affixing hair, an ivory bodkin, silver tweezers to remove any little hair that might appear, a quicksilver mirror to make up her face, and a cloth to clean it off with spittle.

After all this, they begin to get into the ointments, little vials, pots and saucers where they keep cosmetics, some to tighten the skin, others to make it shine, and marrow of deer, cow and sheep. Worse than devils are these women, who make soap with the fat of deer kidneys; they filter water through raw hemp and sarmentum ash, and when the kidney fat is melted on the fire, they add it to the water when there is a very strong sun, stirring it for nine days, an hour each day, until it congeals and becomes what they call Neapolitan soap. Into it they mix musk and civet, cloves steeped two days in orange blossom water, or orange blossoms, to anoint their hands, which become as soft as silk. They have a cosmetic to tighten the skin of women whose breasts and hands are becoming wrinkled. A third cosmetic, which the wretches make from sublimate of silver and May water, the stone being ground nine times and nine days

---

[1] I have not been able to find the meaning of this word.

with a very little quicksilver, and afterwards cooked until a third of it is lost, is such a strong cosmetic that it is not fit to write about. That of the second boiling is used to smooth wrinkles on the breast and face. They also make a liquid from the whites of cooked eggs, distilled with myrrh, camphor, *angelores*, [1] turpentine purified in three waters and well washed so it is as white as snow, roots of white lilies, fine borax; from all this they make a cosmetic with which they shine like a sword. And from cooked egg yolks they prepare a lotion for their hands; they bring them to the fire in a pan and sprinkle them with rose water, and they remove the oil with a clean cloth and two sticks, to soften and purify their hands and face.

I am not telling this so they will do it, for if they do not know about it from somewhere else they will not learn it by reading it here; but I am telling it so they will be aware that their secrets and tricks are known...

All the evil lies in the fact that woman is conceited to an excessive degree; for there is not a woman in the world, for the most part, who can refrain from boasting and priding herself on her finery and beauty, and who does not believe all the words that are said in her praise, even though they are not true, presuming that she is as people say. I am not surprised that this blemish is found in females, for it comes to them naturally from our mother Eve, who believed the serpent, the devil Satan, who came to deceive her, telling her, "If you eat of the fruit of this tree of the knowledge of good and evil, you will be equal to the Almighty who made you." Then, through the weakness of her understanding and with great vanity, believing that Lucifer was equal in knowledge to Him whose wisdom has no peer, and that being equal to Him in knowledge, she would be equal to Him in power, she committed that which was forbidden, she tasted. And so did man and woman come to their fall, to which state they brought their descendants, for women were, are still and will be the same, an example of vanity in wishing to be great, powerful and truly feared... I tell you, moreover, that there is not a woman today who could get her fill of being looked at, desired and sighed after, praised and spoken of by the people. This is her desire, this is her insistence, this is completely her god,

---

[1] unknown word.

pleasure, joy and gladness. Therefore, their whole life is to go out and appear dressed-up, with as much vanity and pomp as each can muster; and when people look at them, sigh for them or talk about them or call them names in the street, they act disdainful, as if angered, and give people a cold stare, showing little patience; but· God knows the truth, that they are like the kicks of a mule, for they would like people never to do anything but desire, talk about and even sneer at them. And although they say, "Did you ever see such a fool? Look at the madman! Did you see such a simpleton?" and say it with outward calm, under their cloaks they are laughing like mad. And when a good-looking woman is in a place where she is not gaped at, she bursts and dies; but when she is where people look at her, you would not recognize her; she makes more bows and gestures than a new jouster. All this comes from vanity and pride.

A daughter says to her mother, a wife to her husband, a sister to her brother, a cousin to her cousin, a mistress to her boy friend: "Oh, how vexed I am! My head aches, my body hurts all over, my stomach is out of sorts, from being closed up between these walls. I want to go to the indulgences; I want to go to St. Francis'; I want to go to mass at St. Dominic's; they are presenting a passion play at the Carmelites'; let's go see the monastery of St. Augustine. Oh, what a pretty monastery! Let's go by the church of the Trinity to see the helmet of St. Blas; let's go to St. Mary's; let's see how those fat abbots walk about (I swear, they have fat necks and are rich and well dressed!); let's go to St. Mary's of Grace and hear the sermon." They propose all these outings and others, according to where they live, in order to be seen and looked at. And the worst is that some women do not have the finery with which to go out, nor women and maids to accompany them, so they say: "Mary, dear, go to my cousin's house and have her lend me her red skirt. Jennie, go to my sisters, to borrow her cloak, the green one of Florentine silk. Agnes, honey, go to my friend's house and borrow her hair net and her bracelet. Katie, go to my neighbor's and ask her to lend me her belt and her gold earrings. Frances, my pet, you go to Mrs. Whats-her-name's and borrow her gold rosary. Terry, dear, run over to my niece's house and borrow her cloak, the one lined with marten fut. Mencihuela, hop over to the perfumer's or the shopkeeper's and bring me some corrosive sublimate, and two ounces of cinnamon and cloves to keep in my mouth."

These and other things do they borrow, more or less according to what each has and her station in life; some borrow more, some less. Some lack a single thing, and others more than four, and still others the entire finery that they are to show off; and they even borrow servant women and maids. And if she wants to ride, the mule is borrowed, as are a lad to hold up her train, two, three or four footmen around her to keep her from falling, and they in the mud up to their knees, freezing with the cold or sweating like pigs in the summer from fatigue, running after her mule or along side it, propping her up, while she is making gestures as if she were tilting in a tourney, and signalling that they should approach to hold her, and she puts one hand on one man's shoulders and the other on another's head; her arms spread out like the wings of a brooding hen about to take off; rising up in the saddle when she sees that people are looking at her, making sorrowful grimaces, sometimes complaining and other times groaning, saying: "Look out, I'm falling! Oh, what a bad saddle! Oh, what a bad mule; it has a difficult gait. I'm all worn out; it trots instead of walking. My hand hurts from pulling on the reins, oh wretched me! It has me all tired out. What will become of me?" And she goes along weeping like a martyr.

But if some squire is leading her mount by the reins and there are people who might look at her, she says: "Oh, my friends, straighten this skirt for me! Adjust this stirrup! Oh, how the saddle twists! She does this so they will stop there a bit with her and she can be gawked at. All this is done with vanity, pride and arrogance...

> (Alonso Martínez de Toledo, *El Corbacho*, from chapters 2, 3, and 9 of Part II)

FESTIVITIES AND AMUSEMENTS

Life was not all warfare, politics or struggle for the nobles of the fifteenth century. Festivities were frequent and at times quite elaborate. But even here, the main activity seems to have been jousting, to judge by the accounts of contemporary writers. For one such account we again resort to the *Crónica del Halconero*, which tells about a series of festivities held in Valladolid in 1428. Prince Enrique of Aragon (son of Fernando de Antequera) arranged the first entertainment. His brother Juan, King of Navarre, provided the second. A third festivity (not included here because it is so similar to the preceding) was offered by their cousin, the King of Castile. There is an assurance of accuracy in the Falconer's account because he, Pedro Carrillo de Huete, was one of the judges for the joust held by Prince Enrique. The elaborateness of the preparation of the mock fortress and tents, the richness of costumes and the rather theatrical nature of the celebrations are evidence of the pleasure seeking court life under Juan II.

Concerning the festivities that Prince Enrique held in Valladolid.

On Tuesday, May 18, in the year of our Lord 1428, in the city of Valladolid, Prince Enrique held a very notable festival in the following manner.

In the square of the city, on the corner of the street that runs from the *Puerta del Campo* to the square, he set up a fortress made of wood and canvas. It was constructed like this: a very tall tower, with four turrets around the top; over the ground floor of the tower a belfry was made and a bell hung therein; and above the belfry was a column, made in the same manner as the tower, which looked like stone. On top of the column was a gilded griffin which held in its paws a large white and red banner. Each of the four turrets above the tower had its small standard, just like the large one.

The tower was surrounded by a high wall, with four towers, and then a parapet a little lower than the wall with twelve more towers. In each of these towers was a well dressed lady. Down below, on the ground floor of the fortress, were provided dressing rooms for the Prince and stables for the horses.

Lists for jousting with canes were set up, which began at the fortress and at the other end had two more towers and an archway, through which all the knights-errant were to come. Letters on this arch said: "This is the arch of the dangerous passage to Formidable Venture."

In each of these two towers was a man with a huntsman's horn. When it was all completed, the fortress and towers looked like they were made of stone masonry. Over the scaffolding of the wall, adjacent to the tower, was a large golden wheel, which was termed the "wheel of Fortune." At the foot of the wheel was a very rich place to sit. After all this was established in good order, my lord the Prince came forth as defender of the lists, in royal trappings and with five other knights whom he brought with him; these were Juan Manrique, son of Garci Fernández Manrique, Friar Gutierre de Cárdenas, Lope de Hoyos, Alvaro de Sandoval and Diego de Tejeda.

But before he came forth in his armor, the Prince arrived at the fortress with many gentlemen of his household, and danced a while at the base of the fortress. Afterwards they brought out many hens, kids and sheep, and they [ate and] drank. Then the Prince mounted his horse and rode to his chambers.

Next he brought an entertainment that arrived in this fashion. Eight damsels, well and beautifully dressed, came on handsome chargers, all with ther caparisons. Then came a goddess on a wagon, with twelve damsels, all singing, and many musicians. They seated the goddess on that throne at the foot of the wheel, with the other damsels around her. In the towers over the gate to the fortress were many gentlemen, all wearing surcoats with silver embroidery, the livery that the Prince had given out.

Then the Prince and his knights donned their armor in his fortress. And as some knights were approaching the "arch of the dangerous passage," those who were in the archway towers sounded their horns, and a lady rang the bell she had in the fortress. At this, a damsel came forth from the fortress on a small horse, accompanied by a herald, and asked:

"Cavaliers, what chance has brought you to this dangerous passage, which is called 'the passage of Formidable Venture'? It would behoove you to go back, for you cannot pass without a contest."

They replied that they were ready for that. From among them rode forth the King of Castile, with twenty-four knights, all in their green serrated trimmings; and the King wore trappings of gold embroidery work with rich ermine trim, and a large plume and crown of butterflies.

The King broke two strong staves and was such a skillful knight that it was astounding, for no one else was so good. Next, the King of Navarre came forth with twelve knights, all dressed like windmills. And the King of Navarre broke one stave.

Gonzalo de Cuadros ran against the Prince, who was defending, and broke a strong stave, and the Prince went down on the lists for such a long time that people though he was dead. Next, a squire of the Prince's, who was defending with him, ran against Ruy Díaz de Mendoza, chief steward of the King of Castile, and in this encounter his bile burst within his body, and he died two hours later. The name of this squire was Alvaro de Sandoval.

After night-fall the Kings, the Queen and the Princes went to sup with the Prince at the dwelling of don Alfonso Enriques, Admiral of Castile. And they all slept there.

The judges of this joust were Diego de Ribera, *adelantado* of Andalusia, Rodrigo de Perea, *adelantado* of Cazorla, Pedro Carrillo de Huete, chief falconer of the King, and Juan Carrillo de Toledo.

On the festivity given by the King of Navarre.

Monday, the 24th of May, in the year of our Lord 1428, in the city of Valladolid, my lord the King of Navarre held another festivity. He had a tent set up with two alcoves and two main halls, and he held the lists in royal harness, with five other knights, all of whom wore trappings with tassled gorgets.

The King of Navarre brought thirteen pages, all with gorgets worked in silver embroidery and wearing pointed scarlet caps. He conducted himself like a wonderful knight, worked harder than any of those who were defending with him, and broke more staves.

Then the King of Castile came forth with ten knights, all in trappings of brown arabesque work and graceful panaches. My lord the King wore a javelin over his shoulder and a horn on his back, and all the knights with him were armed with their hunting lances on their shoulders and their horns. The King brought in front of him a very strong lion and a bear, with many huntsmen and dogs that went along barking.

The King made a tour of the lists and then ran two courses; one carried off the crest of a helmet and the other broke a very strong stave. And all those who were with him broke their staves in a handsome manner.

Next, Prince Enrique came out with five knights, all with coverings of thick brown and blue wool. The Prince broke one stave
and returned to his lodging. He at once came back, again armed,
but alone on his horse and without any trumpeter, wearing very
rich adornments embroidered in gold. This embroidery was in the
shape of spheres, with some bands which had letters saying
"Non es."

Afterwards, the King set up in a garden near his lodging a
great hall, which must have been two hundred feet long and sixty
feet wide, the walls of which were all French tapestries, and the
roof was a red, white and blue cloth, with a drapery across one
end of the hall. The King of Castile, the Queen, the Prince and
the Princesses supped there. While they were eating, many gentlemen
jousted in war harness. And they all slept there.

(Pedro Carrillo de Huete, *Crónica del
Halconero de Juan II*, chapters 3 and 5).

PLAYING CARDS

A quieter type of amusement was card playing. Unfortunately, no Castilian source that I know reveals anything about the games that must have been played at this
time, but there is a work which shows what a deck of cards
was like. This is the *Libro de las veinte cartas e questio-
nes (Book of twenty letters and questions)* by Fernando
de la Torre.

The author's life is not well known. He was an inhabi-
tant of Burgos, studied in Florence, served in the court
of Navarre, travelled in France and was a guard and
vassal of the King of Castile. He lived well into the reign
of Juan II's successor, Enrique IV. Among his friends, with
whom he exchanged poetry and letters, were the outstanding literary men of the time, the Marquis of Santillana,
Pero López de Ayala and Alfonso de Cartagena, the Bishop of Burgos. At the death of the latter, de la Torre wrote
a moving letter expressing his admiration for the Bishop
and grief at his loss.

The *Libro de las veinte cartas* was dedicated to the
Countess of Foix in 1446. It is composed of twenty chapters of prose and verse, and the subject matter ranges from

consolatory letters to questions and answers concerning philosophy, religion and erudition. The nineteenth chapter describes a deck of cards that the author designed for the Countess of Castañeda. The deck consisted of one card called the "Emperor" and four suits of twelve cards each, three face cards —king, knight and knave or jack— and nine number cards. Each card had a poem composed by de la Torre: a twelve line stanza for the king, eleven lines for the knight, ten for the knave, etc., down to the one card which had a single verse. The cards were hand-painted and the following are the poet's instructions to the artist:

The pattern of the designs and histories for the painter is this. First: he is to place all the stories and designs above the verses, which are to be in the middle of the card, properly arranged according to the length of the poem; and beneath the poem, a sign of a heart, spade, diamond or club, depending on the card, and around all the poems and designs, foliage to fill out the card. The backs of all should be blue or green, and not white.

The story or design of the "Emperor", above the verses, is to be like my lady the Countess of Castañeda, richly dressed and on her knees hearing mass, with a female dwarf who is giving her a book, and on her back, an escutcheon with her coat-of-arms, which is two castles and a lion, the arms of the Enriques. With her should be a damsel praying in a book, and on her back, another smaller shield with the same coat-of-arms, except that it should have a bar across; and with her, another lady praying with a rosary.

The design of the king of spades is to be an abbess of the Order of St. Bernard or the Convent of Las Huelgas, with miter and staff, as she and her nuns are gathered around a royal tomb, reading a memorial; and in the middle of the tomb, an escutcheon with the royal arms of castles and lions.

The design of the knight is to be how our lord the King comes on horseback to the aforementioned convent and dismounts in the yard of elm trees, where he is received by the abbess and her convent in procession, without miter and staff, but simply, with a cross before them.

The design of the jack is to be how all the gentlemen, nuns and damsels stroll through the cloister two by two.

The design of the king of hearts is to be the story of Lucrecia, wearing a crown, and how a knight enters her room at night to rape her, and afterwards, how he is killed for this and she commits suicide with a sword.

The design of the knight is to be how a knight of Cordoba comes on horseback to his home, enters on foot and finds with his wife in her chamber two knight commanders, one of the Order of Alcántara with a green cross and the other of the Order of Calatrava with a red cross; and with his sword he kills them, his wife and two other damsels.

The jack is to have as its design how Paris stole Helen from the temple of Diana on the island of Cythera.

The design of the king of clubs is to be the story of Queen Penthesilea, with a crown, and with her some Amazons in war garb who come to help Hector.

The design of the knight is to be the story of Judith, how she kills Prince Holofernes, who is on horseback.

The design of the jack is to be the story of Queen Dido, how she throws herself on the great fire.

The design of the king of diamonds is to be the story of the enchanted damsel, how she is in the lake, rearing Launcelot; she wears a crown.

The design of the knight is to be the story of Gismunda, how her father sends her a gentleman on horseback, who brings her the heart of her lover, Ricardo, which she drinks with certain herbs in a gold goblet, and dies.

The design of the jack is to be the story of how Vidus swam the sea to see his beloved Merus, who is in a tower on an island, and how the storm kills him and brings his dead body to the foot of that tower, and how she, seeing him, kills herself with a sword.

Around all the designs and poems there should be foliage to fill out the card. There should also be foliage around all the other cards that are not face cards.

(Fernando de la Torre, *Libro de las veinte cartas e quistiones,* chapter 19).

TRAVEL

Another outlet for the adventurous spirit of fifteenth century Spaniards was travel. Events within the country created a great deal of movement, and the court itself was peripatetic. But people also voyaged beyond the borders of the Peninsula, either in the service of king and church or to satisfy their personal desires to see the world. The Council of Basel, for instance, was attended by a large, and changing, delegation of Spanish clerics and noblemen. Among individual travellers were such well known figures as Gutierre Quixada, Diego de Valera or Pero Niño. Quixada, who took part in the *Paso Honroso* of Suero de Quiñones, was famous as a jouster and travelled to Burgundy to exhibit his prowess. He also made a pilgrimage to the Holy Land. Valera travelled extensively in central Europe, being received with pomp and honor in places like Bohemia and Burgundy. Pero Niño, whose chronicle is utilized several times in this collection, spent considerable time in France and on the high seas. It should also be noted that the kingdom of Aragon, blocked within the Peninsula by the expansion of Castile, turned seaward and in 1442 its king, Alfonso V, triumphantly entered the city of Naples. He set up his court there and travel between Spain and Italy was constant.

One voyager has left a particularly worthwhile account of his activities, *Las andanzas e viajes de Pero Tafur (The travels and voyages of Pero Tafur)*. This author was a young, noble and cultured knight of the court who, provided with plenty of money and letters of recommendation from his sovereign, set out in the autumn of 1435. For three and a half years he made a "grand tour", passing along the Moroccan coast, the south and east coast of Spain and thence to Italy. After visiting Florence, Pisa and Venice, he proceeded east to the Holy Land, Egypt, Cyprus, Rhodes and Constantinople. Back in Italy, he went north through Switzerland, Germany and Flanders and returned to his native country, again by way of Italy. Tafur had a sharp eye and an inquisitive nature, and what he saw, heard and did is recorded in detail, sometimes with credulity, but almost always interestingly.

For inclusion here I have selected that part of his travels that brought him to the Holy Land; a visit to the region where Jesus lived and died was the most important and difficult of the three main pilgrimages that medieval

for men and others for women. We spent a day there. The next morning we went two miles on, to the monastery of St. George, where they say his body is buried, and they also say that he killed the dragon there, although many people are of the opinion that he killed it in Beirut, the port of Damascus. This day we went to sleep five leagues from there, near a castle called Emmaus. Early the following morning we left and travelled another five leagues to the city of Jerusalem. Some of its buildings, such as Mount Sion, the Castles of King David and the Holy Sepulcher, which is a very tall chapel, can well be seen from a distance of four leagues. As we arrived, all the Christians, Greeks as well as the other nations, came out to receive us and took us to a large square in front of the Holy Sepulcher. There we said prayers, but they would not let us go inside. We were taken to the lodging that the previously mentioned Godfrey of Bouillon made, where we found an abundance of foods of many kinds, which the Greeks prepare to sell to the Christians. Later the Guardian of Mount Sion came, accompanied by his friars, and took ten or twelve of us gentlemen to his monastery, for such is his custom, and lodged us very well. From that day on he gave us, who were staying there, two friars to accompany and tell us about the things we were to see in Jerusalem and its territory. This Mount Sion is a monastery on the highest point at one end of the city and has many places where our Lord worked many miracles. There is a tall tower, in the cavern of which our Lord appeared in fire to all the assembled disciples —this is the Feast of the Holy Ghost—, and from there one can see the Sea of Sodom and Gomorrah, which they call Pentapolis (which means "five cities"). In the bottom part of the tower is a chapel, where our Lord appeared to the Apostle Saint Thomas, when He told him to put his hand in His side, and many other things happened in that house. At the entrance to it, a street away, is the house of the Virgin Mary, and further on, at the back of the monastery, is the place where our Lord supped with His disciples. We rested there this day; the next, we went to hear mass at the Holy Sepulcher, which is only opened once a year. They counted us there, according to the document we had been given in Jaffa, and they received seven and a half ducats from each pilgrim. With the two that were paid for the animals in Jaffa, and with certain *gruessos* that are paid at the sanctuaries —eleven *gruessos* are worth a ducat—, twelve and a half ducats in fees are paid by each person. When we entered the Holy Sepulcher, there came forth in a procession to receive us the Christians who had been shut up there for the past year, to wit: the Catholics —three friars of St. Francis who were there—, the Greeks, the Jacobites, the Armenians, the Nestorians, those from India, and the Coptics, in short, seven kinds of Christians. We went with the precession first to the Holy Sepulcher, which is a large, very tall chapel covered with lead, at the top of which is a large opening through which the light enters, and in the middle of it is a small chapel, and in that chapel still a smaller one, and there is the Holy Sepulcher. It is so narrow that only the person saying mass and one other, who serves, can fit into it. We said our prayers there and set out, in order, with the procession for Mount Calvary, where our Lord was crucified. This must be twelve or fifteen paces from there, and is a high rock covered with a chapel very richly worked in mosaic; there is the hole in the rock where the cross of our Lord was placed, and the other two holes for the thieves. Having said our prayer, we descended to the place where our Lord was anointed. From there we went to where our Lord was arrested, when they wished to crucify Him, and then we went to the place where St. Helen found the cross of Jesus Christ, and then to where our Lord put His finger, saying that here was half of the world. Next we went to a place that the friars have, where all the relics are kept, and where our Lord appeared to the holy Mary Magdalene in the guise of a gardener. At the entrance is a large hall, hung with many pennants and flags of Christian kings and princes, and the gentlemen who go to that place hang up their coats-of-arms there. All these things and many more are within this cemetery; all the holy relics are here, and each Christian sect mentioned above has its own sanctuary. After the procession was over and we had heard mass, we went to eat, for the Greeks had a well prepared meal for us, for our money. This day the Arabs and Christians are permitted to set out goods to sell to us. We stayed there that day and night, hearing the divine offices, which each of these nations celebrates in a different way. Here is the tomb of Duke Godfrey of Bouillon, with letters carved on a stone that say: "Hic iacet inclitvs Godefroidvs de Bvlion qvi totem istam terram acqvisivit cultvi Christiano, cvivs anima cvm Christo reqviescat amen."

Next to it is the tomb of his brother, King Baldwin, in the same fashion, and it says: "Rex Baldeqinvs Ivdas alter Machabevs spes patriae vigor ecclae virtvs vtrivsque qvem formidabant cvi dona ferebant cedar Aegypti dan ac homicida Damascvs proh dolor in modico clavditvr hoc tvmvlo."

The next day, after we heard mass, they opened the door for us and checked us out by number, and sent us to our lodging. This day we went to see the cemetery and valley of Josaphat, where the sepulcher of the Virgin Mary is, in an underground vault fifteen or twenty steps down. Two friars of St. Francis are on guard there. We paid certain *gruessos*. Next we went to the garden where our Lord was arrested, and then up to the Mount of Olives, whence He ascended into heaven. There is a notable church there, and on a stone slab is the shape of His foot. We proceeded to the place where the assembled disciples made the Credo, and then to where our Lord composed the Pater Noster. Nearby is the alder tree on which Judas hanged himself. Returning to the city of Jerusalem, we passed the place where the wood of the cross was kept for a long time. Near it is the scene of the stoning of St. Stephen. We entered near the Golden Gate, which is right next to the temple of Solomon, and we passed the pool where the angel stirred up the water with which he cured the sick. From here we visited the houses of Pontius Pilate and Caifas, and in the place where Jesus Christ was judged, people are now condemned to death. We went along the street that is called the Street of Sorrow, where our Lord carried the cross on His back. It is covered with terraces, and the rainwater that is gathered there goes to the cistern from which the people of the city drink, for there is a great scarcity of water. This day we went to rest at our lodgings. The next morning we left Jerusalem with the Governor and the friars and went to Bethlehem, which is five leagues away. On the way we were shown a chapel, where the star appeared again to the three Magi, and about a league further on we came to the house of the prophet Elias. We reached Bethlehem, a little town of some fifty inhabitants, at noon. The Arabs showed as much reverence there as we did, and we entered the monastery, which is very notable, large and with rich buildings. Six friars are always there, and they came out in procession to greet us. Then they led us into a low, undergound chapel where our Lord was born. Nearby is the manger, and at the exit to that cave, the place where He was circumcised. From there we went to the caves where the Innocents were buried; in those caves is the dwelling where St. Jerome translated the Bible. We stayed there that day and paid certain *gruessos*. After mass the following day, we set out for the place where St. John the Baptist was born, which is five leagues distant. St. Zachariah lived there and composed the psalm, "Benedictus Dominus Deus Israel." It is a great sanctuary. We spent the whole day there and the next day returned to Jerusalem, three leagues distant, arriving early. That day we went to visit some sanctuaries in Jerusalem: the house of St. Ann; the house where St. Peter denied Jesus Christ (the stone with which Christ was covered in the sepulcher is there); the house of St. James the Greater, and that of St. James the Lesser; the grave of Absalom, which is outside the citiy —right around the time we were there, it is said that some Arabs, looking for treasure, heard a voice there and were taken out dead—; a fountain that our Lady the Virgin Mary is said to have brought forth; the spot where our Lord fell with the cross; the castles of King David; the house where our Lord washed the disciples' feet; and many more holy places. We rested the next day, and on the following morning left Jerusalem with the Governor and the friars and went to the castle and town of Magdala (which was the property of the Magdalene) to eat. There is a fine church there, and the place where our Lord revived Lazarus, and other holy places. We paid certain *gruessos*. We left in the afternoon and visited a place that belonged to St. Martha, the sister of the Magdalene. That night we went to sleep at a house on a mountain where our Lord cured many sick people that were brought to Him. The next morning we travelled to Jericho, which is reckoned at fifteen leagues from Jerusalem. It is a very long valley and large lowland, through which passes the River Jordan, to the place where our Lord baptized St. John and was baptized by him. A stone masonry cross is set up within the water as a memorial. We all bathed there; a gentleman from Germany drowned that day. This is a place of great devotion. The pilgrims were to return to Jericho to sleep that night and continue the next day to the Mount of Lent, where our Lord fasted. I asked an Arab to take me to the Arabian Desert, which is about three leagues away, to where St. John had gone about preaching, and where St. Anthony, the first hermit, and other holy fathers had lived. From there he brought me back by way of the Sea of Pentapolis (this means the five cities —Sodom, Gomorrah and three others— that were destroyed for the sin of sodomy). The water is so fetid that I could not describe it. No fish lives in it and it is even said that a bird will refuse to alight on it. The Arab who took me told me a very marvelous thing: that the River Jordan enters into the sea and flows out the other side without mingling with the other water, and he says that in the middle of the sea one can drink sweet water from the river. All around that valley grow some tall, thin trees, loaded with a fruit something like grapefruit, and if you bring your fingers near it, no matter how gently, it inmediately breaks and fumes come out, and the odor sticks to your hand all day. The next day I went back to eat in Jericho, which is a village of some hundred inhabitants. I took from there some of those roses of Jericho that are placed on women in childbirth. Many holy places where our Lord walked were shown to me. On that side of the river is a province called Trans-Jordan Bethany. I went to sleep that night at the mount where our Lord fasted, and there I found the Christians. It is a high range, in the middle of which are some small chapels and a road built along the rock, to get to it, all of which St. Helen had constructed to honor that holy place. On the way up, a squire from Galicia, trying to help a lady, fell head-long from the mountain and was smashed to pieces when he hit the bottom. It is quite a fearful place to go up. We descended right away and by an easier road went up to the highest point, where the Devil tempted our Lord. From there we came down to a fountain, where the people of Jericho had brought many foods to sell to us. We remained there all that night. The next morning we took that body and carried it to the house which I have said was on the mount, and there we buried it and spent the entire day. The following morning we returned to the castle of Magdala. The Governor remained behind, hunting, and entrusted us to one of his knights, who accompanied us as far as the church where Lazarus was revived. The *alcaide* of the region demanded certain tribute from us, and the Arab who was accompanying us replied that it would not be paid, for it never had been the custom. The argument became so heated that the *alcaide* and his men took to their weapons against our knight and even wounded him. We hastened to his aid and wounded a good number of the Arabs and seized the *alcaide* and some

of his men, and took them before the Governor, who was coming
just then. He investigated the affair and ordered the *alcaide* killed
—his head was cut off immediately— and the prisoners lashed.
We remained there until the evening and went to Jerusalem to
sleep. The following day we set out with the same people and
went to another Bethany, from where we were shown many holy
places, including Mount Tabor, where our Lord was transfigured,
and they say that here is the valley of Hebron, where the graves
of Adam and Eve are. We returned to Jerusalem that night, passing holy places and the garden where our Lord prayed and where
He was arrested. We arrived in Jerusalem early. That night, I
offered a renegade Arab, who was a native of Portugal, two ducats
to take me to see the temple of Solomon, and he did so. I went
in with him, dressed in his clothes, at one o'clock at night, and
saw all the temple, which is a single nave, all worked in gold mosaic, with the floor and walls of very beautiful white tiles, and so
many hanging lamps that they seem to touch each other, and the
ceiling overhead all smooth and covered with lead. In truth, they
say that when Solomon built this, it was the best structure in
the world; it was later destroyed and rebuilt, but certainly it is
one of the fine buildings in the world today. If I had been recognized as a Christian there, I would have been dead on the spot.
A short time ago this temple was a holy church, but a favorite
of the Sultan's had such influence with him that he took it and
changed it into a mosque. That renegade Arab who took me there
brought me back to Mount Sion, where the friars were waiting
for me, fearing I might be dead, since I was so late in coming.
They were very happy at my arrival, and no less so were the knights
with whom I was travelling. That night we arranged to go to hear
mass and spend the whole next day and night at the Holy Sepulcher. We went at sunrise and the door was opened for us with all
the same ceremony as before. We all confessed and took commun-
ion that day, and I armed three knights, two Germans and one
Frenchman. We put our arms in the accustomed place and picked
from among the relics that the Guardian offered us. We heard
mass at dawn the following day and left. All this day and the
following two, we did nothing but visit holy places and buy some
things and prepare for our departure. All this time I had been looking for a way to go to St. Catherine's on Mount Sinai, which is

near the Red Sea. I discovered that the dragomen and camels had already left with an ambassador of the Turk, who was going to the Sultan in Cairo. For this reason my trip was prevented; I would have liked to stay there, if necessary, until the next year, but the Guardian advised me to go to Cyprus, where I would find the Cardinal, the brother of the old king, and he would find a way for me to go to Cairo, and from there to Mount Sinai, and I followed his advice. The next day we left with the Governor and the friars and went to Rama to sleep, and the following day to the port of Jaffa, where we found the galleys ready, and embarked. The Arabs and the friars returned to Jerusalem, and we made our way to Beirut. The *adelantado* Nazardin spent this day telling me what had happened to him with the King of Dacia. We went to the port of Damascus and along the coast saw Arsur, Ascalon and Acre, which is a castle to which the Knights of St. John withdrew when they lost Jerusalem. Nearby is Nazareth, in Galilee, where our Lady was hailed by the angel. From there we went down to Beirut, and the skippers took on certain merchandise. I would have liked to go to Damascus, but they refused to wait for me. From there they showed me the Mountain of Lebanon, which is all covered with cedars, which look like laurel trees. People say that St. George killed the dragon in Beirut, and they find them under rocks in the fields, just as we find scorpions, but they do not grow big any more or have poison, it is said, at the request of the blessed St. George. I had good information about the city of Damascus, but since I did not see it, I shall leave it for someone who did.

(Pero Tafur, *Andanzas e viajes*)

SENTIMENTAL LIFE

The Marriage of Pero Niño

Marriage arrangements among the nobility were, for the most part, matters of family alliances and treaties, rather than of personal preference. Children were promised to each other at an early age, as can be seen from the account of the alliances arranged for members of the powerful Manrique family in 1428:

> And in this place [*Turégano*] were signed the marriage agreements, which had been under discussion for many days, between the eldest son of the Count of Castro, who was over thirteen years of age, and the second daughter of the *adelantado* Pedro Manrique, of a similar age, and between the eldest son of this *adelantado,* who was eighteen years old, and a daughter of the Count of Castro, who was not over seven.
>
> They were publicly betrothed in the presence of the King, the King of Navarre and other Grandees who were at court, in the palace of the Queen.
>
> The same night that this betrothal was publicly celebrated, another was made secretly between the eldest son of Pedro de Stúñiga, who must have been over sixteen, and the third daughter of the *adelantado* Pedro Manrique, who was thirteen years old. This betrothal was arranged in secret because the Count of Castro and Pedro de Stúñiga were not on good terms at that time and the *adelantado* did not want the Count of Castro to know about it.
>
> (*Crónica de don Juan II, attributed to Alvar García de Santa María, year 1428, chapter 6*).

Nevertheless, love matches were not unknown. For such a case, we turn to the biography of Pero Niño, the *Victorial* of Gutierre Díez de Games, which tells of the difficulties encountered by the hero and the lady of his choice. She was doña Beatriz, the second daughter of Prince Juan of Portugal (who had fled to Castile from his brother, King Fernando) and his wife, doña Costanza. Because of the wealth and lands she inherited, doña Beatriz was one of the best marriage prospects in the country, and for that reason Prince Fernando, the regent during the minority of Juan II, had her betrothed to his own son, when she was thirteen and the boy a mere three years of age. Later, King Martin of Aragon sought her hand and the Prince Regent, disregarding the previous betrothal to his son, was willing to agree to the match. The King of Aragon married elsewhere, however, and it was at this point that doña Beatriz decided to choose for herself. The events related below took place in 1409, when Pero Niño was about thirty years of age. It was the third love affair of his life, according to his chronicler. The first resulted in his marriage to doña Costanza de Guevara, who died within four or five years of the wedding. While he was in France, he had a gallant, chivalric attachment to Madame de Serifontaine, widow of Renaud de Trie, Admiral of France, which ended by mutual consent. His marriage to doña Beatriz lasted many years, until her death, at the age of sixty, in 1446.

How and for what reason was the beginning whereby Pero Niño was enamoured of the doña Beatriz.

Prince Fernando held great festivities and rejoicings in Valladolid at that time, for the Queen of Navarre, his aunt, had come there, accompanied by honored knights and great lords, and many beatiful ladies and damsels. And there were also many knights, ambassadors from France and England, and Moors from Granada. The Queen, the King's mother, often had jousts held and tilting with reed spears and tourneys on horseback and on foot, and the knights carried on these jousts almost every day. Pero Niño, too, attended the jousting a great deal and when he went to joust, he usually took along four or five knights of his household, armed for the tournaments; but sometimes he went alone and jousted with very strong staves and had several encounters each day, in which he unseated quite a few knights, including some who had unseated other knights.

One day it happened that they were jousting in a street called the *Cascagera,* where the joust was carried on most frequently. Pero Niño took part that day and, among others whom he knocked down, he unseated one of the strongest and greatest knights of the Prince's household. He was such an important knight that I shall refrain from saying who he was. On that street was an honorable abode where the lady doña Beatriz, the daughter of Prince Juan, was staying at the time. With her was her cousin, doña Margarita, the daughter of Count Enrique Manuel. Also present was ... [1], inasmuch as marriage to her was several times discussed with him, and she was a person of such beauty and lineage as well befitted him, but that was not his desire.

It happened that on the day that Pero Niño unseated that great knight of the Prince's household, as is usually the case, some people were sorry and others pleased at his fall. The lady doña Beatriz, her cousin doña Margarita and many other ladies and damsels were watching. And doña Margarita said:

"It is no wonder the rider fell, for his horse fell; the fault is not the rider's but the horse's."

Doña Beatriz said:

"Cousin, you do not judge well, nor is that what you really believe. You know well enough what happened; the fallen knight leaned so much with the weight of his weapons and pulled on the horse's reins so hard, that horse and rider had to fall."

All the other ladies and damsels there were of doña Beatriz' opinion. Other people were present at those words, and among them was a squire of Pero Niño's, in whose house it was that the lady doña Beatriz was staying, and he told his lord everything, as to how the ladies judged it.

At the time I am telling you about, Pero Niño had already taken leave of Madame, the widow of the Admiral of France, the great lady I told you about before, whom he loved when he was in France, and he had already sent to break off with her because of the war against the Moors, according to the conditions they had agreed on and the time she was to wait for him...

Here the author says that the things that are to be, must be and must have a beginning; and this was the beginning of the marriage

---

[1] Blank in the original.

of this lord and lady, for which they first had to go through many hardships.

As that squire was telling Pero Niño the words that doña Beatriz had said, he immediately resolved in his heart to love that damsel, for his honor's sake; although he knew that she was betrothed, he understood that the match was unequal because of their ages. During this time, Pero Niño learned about the affairs of doña Beatriz, and how, because of the changes of plans that the Prince had forced her to make, she had resolved not to take any husband except one she herself wanted.

And as Pero Niño ventured to other things, so did he venture to this. He found a way to send someone to tell her that she was the lady he preferred to serve in all the world, for his honor's sake, and he intended to persist in it until death, for she was as noble as any of the queens of all Spain, and the maiden of best repute and highest lineage, and he asked her to let him call himself her knight and be hers on those occasions that were suitable.

When she heard this message she was very surprised and became flustered and blushed, and gave no reply to the messenger then. And Pero Niño did not cease to gain the good will of those people in her household and near her on whom he knew she relied for advice. He paid them many honors and gave them gifts, without revealing anything of his motive. Of all the people in the household of that lady, there was not one who did not talk of Pero Niño and his deeds. The truth is that he furnished quite enough to talk about. Most of them did not know all the reason, but they had some inkling.

Now they talked so much about him in all the house that doña Beatriz marvelled at it very much. One day, therefore, she called two damsels of her retinue whom she trusted much and said: "Tell me, my friends, who introduced Pero Niño into this household, a man to whom I have never spoken and do not know, except by hearsay? I see that all of you talk about him and praise his deeds and gentility more than any other knight in Castile."

One of the girls replied: "If he were not such a person we would not praise him so much, for without a doubt he is today the flower of all knights in gentility, chivalry and all the good virtues that could be in the best knight in the world."

And the other one said: "This is very true, my lady, and there is even more good in him than people could tell; fortunate will be the woman who is to have such a husband and lord as this, for she will be happy and live in pleasure her life long."

Now the damsels had this good way of speaking, for they had been approached on Pero Niño's behalf by that squire who spoke to them every day. Doña Beatriz said: "Oh, my friends, how you are deceived! I know well that he is one of the most famous knights in the world today, but they tell me that great ladies lose their reputations on his account, and I would not care to be one of them. For you well know that this is the thing I have always been most on guard against; therefore I command you never to speak to me about this again."

Such was her reply that day, and so was it reported to Pero Niño by that squire. But he, who never forgot what he had proposed in his heart, made a great effort to tell her about himself face to face. One day, when she was about to ride out from her lodging, he found a way to approach, and those who were nearby asked him to take the reins of her mount. He did so, for that was the very chance he was looking for. As they went along, he had the opportunity to tell her his entire intention, reminding her that he had sent someone to tell her this, and assuring her that his desire was to love her honestly and loyally, to the honor of both. She replied that men's words were very suspect, but that she would take counsel with some people who ought to loyally advise her and would give him an answer.

Pero Niño did not cease to seek out every good means possible to bring this suit to a happy conclusion. Now the lady doña Beatriz had a brother named don Fernando, a natural son of her father, Prince Juan, a good knight and very much a friend of Pero Niño's in times past. During the period of consideration that doña Beatriz had taken to give her answer, he spoke with her brother, don Fernando, and told him all his purpose and how the business stood. When don Fernando learned it, he seemed pleased thereby and promised his help to Pero Niño, for he understood that it was to his sister's honor, considering the marriages that had been proposed and the dealings that were going on in the Prince's household.

From then on, don Fernando was on Pero Niño's side with his sister, and they talked of many things, past, present and future;

he made greatest mention of the latter, for this was being done without the permission of the Prince, who was with the King at that time, for he was regent of the realm during the minority of the King, his nephew.

All this was related to Pero Niño, as were the hardships, anxieties and even dangers that would arise from it; and the answer was that if he wished to offer himself to them in every way, she was agreed, and considering the kind of knight Pero Niño was, for such a person would carry all these deeds through to safety. She said there was no other knight in the kingdom to whom it pertained to undertake this enterprise, except him. Pero Niño was very pleased to hear this reply, for he had already, with great wisdom, considered himself in the mirror of prudence, where he saw that he was obliged to all these things and many more that might befall him.

The marriage was agreed on by her brother and other persons of authority, and they were betrothed by a priest in the presence of discreet and honest witnesses, people worthy of faith and credence; and pledges, dowry and obligations of towns and vassals, such as befitted her station, were exchanged before those who were desirous of her honor and would serve both parties and keep the secret until the day it should be revealed. Some of them had misgivings about the hardships that would ensue, but when they saw that it was agreed on by the principal parties, they indeed believed it was the will of God and would end well, as it later did.

Henceforward, Pero Niño was much happier than he was before, and kept himself better prepared and in greater style, as one who intended to bring that deed to a successful conclusion. And henceforth he never took much care to keep the matter hidden, but told it to some people and did not conceal it from others who asked about it, so he knew that it had already been spoken about somewhat to the Prince. Before it should go further, he desired to reveal it himself. Since the Prince was eager for war, especially against the Moors, he paid the knight greater honor than anyone else of the same rank, or even higher. Therefore Pero Niño went to him and said:

"My lord, I have been a retainer of King Enrique, your brother, and as your Grace knows, I did him many services on land and sea; and when the time came when he was to give me reward and position, as he had promised, God took him from this world. It is true that when your Grace was left in power, I understood that you would remunerate and reward me for the services I did his Grace, and so I propose to serve you as well as any knight in the world serves king or lord, for which, thanks be to God, I am well prepared. And now, sire, it is necessary for me to take a wife, and I have been offered the best marriages in the kingdom. But since it is my intention to serve you more than all the kings in the world, sire, I am desirous of being your vassal and of marrying in your household."

The Prince replied: "Everything you have said is true, and you may be sure that in everything possible I shall help you as I would the person closest to me who is a retainer in my household. Will you please tell me who it is you desire?"

Then Pero Niño replied that he was somewhat embarrassed to say it personally, but that he would answer through the Prince's confessor. The Prince said he had spoken well.

The next day, Pero Niño gave the confessor an account of the words that had passed between himself and the Prince and told him that the lady was doña Beatriz, the daughter of Prince Juan. It seemed somewhat difficult to the confessor, inasmuch as he knew of several other proposals of marriage that the Prince was entertaining for her outside the realm of Castile, and also that she was not completely free of her betrothal to the Prince's son. Still, he said, he would convey the message and bring back the reply.

Three or four days passed before Pero Niño learned the answer through the confessor, and it was that the Prince ordered and entreated him to speak no more of that marriage, for he had discussed and agreed to her marriage elsewhere, and it was very advantageous to him and could not be broken; but Pero Niño should look anywhere else in the whole kingdom, and he would help him as he had promised; and he would be doing him a great pleasure in this.

Then Pero Niño told the confessor that he should know for certain that if he did not marry that damsel he would never in his life marry another; and if the Prince, certain of this, granted this favor, he would make him the richest knight in the world, and he would serve him for it; if not, he would rather it cost him his head.

The confessor said that, to please him, he would take the message, even though the Prince had spoken very harshly about it.

Henceforth, Pero Niño considered himself free of obligation, since he had made the matter known to the Prince. However, he soon knew hardships and was more on his guard than ever. He always went on horseback, for he was the best man on a horse in the kingdom, and always took along twenty or thirty knights and squires, well prepared and mounted. Now marten furs were not worn so much as was the coat of mail.

Here the author speaks, and treats of fortitude and constancy, of how this knight began the struggle with great spirit and wisdom, fearing neither present nor future blows, but putting aside all hesitation, so as to attain the triumph and honor of this great deed, which he in his heart considered as nothing, as far as the hardships he was to undergo were concerned. See if this was great courage and audacity, that he so fearlessly told such a great prince all his intention, awaited the reply and answered him as you have heard.

After the Prince's reply, Pero Niño spent more than half a year at and near the court, and many times found himself in considerable danger to see his wife. But the things that God desires to be guarded from error are so guarded, for she was as truly disposed to the honor of her lord and husband as any woman in the world could be, as was later to appear. This issue was well known to the Prince and to those around him, who were envious of Pero Niño and impeded him in this affair and in everything else as much as they could; but they were not yet absolutely certain of it. These people were don Sancho de Rojas, Bishop of Palencia, who was afterwards Archbishop of Toledo; Alfonso Enríquez, the Admiral; Count don Enrique Manuel; and Perafán de Ribera, *adelantado* of the frontier; who were the leading men in his council at that time.

Don Ruy López Dávalos, the Constable of Castile, was there and, although he was willing to help Pero Niño, he did not have the opportunity, for everybody thought he had been in on the advice. They did not err much, for although he did not take part in the matter at the beginning, he later helped in it as much as he could. These people kept at the Prince until he felt he had to get at the truth.

*How Pero Niño, with great courage, ventured to tell the
entire deed to the Prince, within his chambers.*

One night Pero Niño was in the palace with the King and
Queen (who had come there from Magaz, where the King was
living), for he was one of his chief guards; and since his affairs
were becoming pressing, it was necessary for him as a knight to
come to see his wife and carry forward his suit, in which his honor
was so much involved. When he had come there, the Prince called
him to his chamber, in the presence of the Bishop of Palencia and
the Constable, to learn from him about this affair which was being
discussed so much. The Prince said that Pero Niño knew well how
he had spoken to him before and that he had replied through his
confessor, beseeching and ordering him to speak no more of this
marriage, but to give it up; and now he had been told that Pero
Niño was saying that doña Beatriz was his wife: and he wanted to
know about it from him.

Pero Niño replied: "Sire, your Grace indeed knows that when
your confessor bade me speak no more of the matter and to forego
this suit, I answered that it was not a thing I could in any wise give
up, for I understood that I was right and that your Grace ought to
be pleased by it for many reasons. First, because it was ordained
by God and our wills were equal, it was a proceeding that no one
should obstruct. The reason was that I considered myself such a
knight as deserved her, having personally done you many note-
worthy services, and I am as ready for this today as any knight
whatsoever. And I entreated you, as earnestly as I could, to please
give her to me, saying you would make me the richest knight in
the world, but that otherwise I would prefer death."

Many words, which would be long to relate here, were spoken
on all this matter; and Pero Niño then departed for Magaz. Many
people in the palace thought that Pero Niño would be arrested at
once, but he spoke so wisely and offered so many good arguments
for himself and presented them with such courage, and the Prince
was so noble and responsive to fairness, that he did not arrest him.
If it were not for evil advisers, he certainly would have given her to
him. The Prince and Princess did not delay in summoning doña
Beatriz. With the Bishop as a witness, they told her that Pero Niño
had said he was her husband, and asked her if this was true.

She was very much afraid that Pero Niño was under arrest, for she knew that he had been in the Prince's palace then; but she learned from a squire that Pero Niño had already departed, so she answered that it was true. They asked her why she had done such a thing, against the Prince's wishes, and having a marriage agreement with his son: and they told her she had committed an ugly thing. She defended herself with many reasons why she had done it; and one, she said, was that she knew perfectly well that when he did not have control of the government of Castile, while his brother the King was alive, he had betrothed her to his son, but now, since he had become regent of the realm, he had discussed other marriages for her outside the kingdom, some to her honor and others less so. Therefore, she was resolved to marry only the person she desired.

And now, relatives of hers and others who were mindful of her honor had brought her that knight, to whom she was betrothed, and very happily so; and she begged him to be pleased thereat, for he would be doing her a great favor. She said that she had done what was right, and she was certain that Pero Niño was such a good knight that the Prince would be well served by him.

The Prince bade her not to speak of that, and he said that great hardships would befall her because of this action. She replied that she was ready to endure all the hardships that might come to her. Then he ordered her not to return to her dwelling, but to remain there with her cousin, the Princess.

The next day, the Prince sent the Bishop of Segovia and Pedro de Monsalvo, the King's treasurer, to the Queen, who was in Magaz with the King, to complain bitterly to her about Pero Niño, saying he had become betrothed to doña Beatriz, even though she was betrothed to his son. And they offered many reasons why Pero Niño should be arrested and why the Queen should hand him over to prison. The Queen had known of the matter for some days and was aiding Pero Niño, but she neither could nor dared to do as much as she would have liked.

Then she called the knight before the ambassadors, and he admitted that it was true that he was betrothed to her, and set forth many reasons why he had done it. He said that the Prince was not his lord, and if he disliked him, and if there were some people in his household who were displeased by his actions and said he had erred and should accept that request, he would fight them before the King, his lord, and before the Queen and the Prince, while doña Beatriz looked on. They could choose two of their number, whomever the Prince or they desired, for he would give them satisfaction as the law of chivalry demands in such a case, in combat from sunrise to sunset, and he would conquer them one by one, and when he had finished with one, he would take on the battle with the other. He said he would kill or throw them from the field and make them confess that he had not erred in becoming betrothed to his wife, doña Beatriz, and that she had not erred either; and his condition was that when the battle to which he offered himself was over, the King should give him his wife, free and without hindrance, right there before everyone. He ended his argument by offering to give the knights who would undertake the enterprise two thousand *doblas* apiece, for a horse each.

With the consent of the Queen, the ambassadors left him with this reply and returned to the Prince. They did not tarry, but returned the following day, and the reply was this: that he would not be given that pleasure, but would be taken care of in a more vexing fashion. Then they discussed with the Queen how he should be arrested, for if he were not, the Prince would come in person.

The Queen lived in constant fear that the King, her son, would be taken away from her. Therefore, she summoned Pero Niño and told him she was well aware that he was a retainer of King Enrique and of the King, her son, and she had seen the hardships he endured every day in guarding and defending the King, her son, and that for this reason the Prince might come to Magaz and seize him there. She said that she would be very saddened at this, not being able to prevent it. She therefore beseeched him to go to the castle of Palenzuela, which Pero Niño held at that time, and in the meanwhile she would do everything possible for his honor. Pero Niño, when he saw that the Queen was right and could do no more, left for Palenzuela, where he stayed several days.

On the day he left Magaz, the Prince sent Diego Fernández de Vadillo to him at Villamediana, where he was stopping, to find out all these things about him; and he reported them back. Then Pero Niño left there for Palenzuela. The Prince had sent men after him and they were in certain places he passed through, but did not dare attack, so he arrived in Palenzuela. The third day he was there, the

Queen sent Rodrigo de Perea, *adelantado* of Cazorla, and García Hurtado, one of the King's macebearers, to tell and command him to go thence, indicating he should take himself to Bayonne in Gascony, for she could not defend him. She sent a letter by this knight, Rodrigo de Perea, a retainer in the King's household and a highly esteemed person, and García Hurtado, the macebearer, also a retainer and official of the King's house, for the law commands that no nobleman may leave the kingdom without dispute, unless by command of the King or some just impediment, for which such a command was necessary. Otherwise he would not have left.

Now the history stops talking about Pero Niño, of how he went to Bayonne and the many hardships and dangers he faced on the road, to tell of his wife, the lady doña Beatriz.

How the lady doña Beatriz was held in the castle of Urueña.

Doña Beatriz remained at that time in the Prince's chambers, where they alternately frightened and flattered her, urging her to give up this suit of Pero Niño's, and they would give her other marriages right then and there; against these arguments she always held fast, saying she would have no husband but Pero Niño, and that on this score she would suffer death, if necessary.

From there the Prince sent her to Urueña, with ladies and damsels to accompany and honor her. There she remained, her honor always respected and very much guarded, so that no man could talk to her, lest Pero Niño should carry her off. In the year and a half that she was there, Pero Niño came to see her and could have carried her away three or four times if he had wished, but he never wanted to have her except in an honorable manner, as he afterwards did.

While Pero Niño was in Bayonne, the Prince was approached by several knights who were friends of Pero Niño's, and by the Queen, who interested herself in this, and by others who charged his conscience, showing him that such a knight was not to be lost, for knights as good as Pero Niño could be found in few places. They also argued that he would be well received in other kingdoms, should he choose to go there. And the Prince indeed had need of him for the war he was waging against the Moors. For these and other reasons, he had to pardon and grant him permission to return to the kingdom of Castile, and he gave him his wife as well as other favors and help.

In the end he was able to win him over; and if the Prince had lived longer, Pero Niño would have found favor with him. When Pero Niño came to Castile, the Queen showed him many favors and received him in that rank in the King's guard that he enjoyed before. He celebrated his wedding in a town of his named Cigales, and remained henceforth at court, until the King was of age. There were many upheavals at court, after the death of Prince don Fernando (who had become King of Aragon); in these affairs Pero Niño bore himself as well as he did in all other things.

(Gutierre Díez de Games, *El Victorial,* chapters 92 to 94.)

INTELLECTUAL LIFE

SUPERSTITIONS

To indicate one aspect of the mentality of the period, I have chosen a passage from the *Tratado de la adivinanza (Treatise on divination)* by Fray Lope de Barrientos (1382-1469), an eminent member of the Dominican Order. After studying philosophy and theology at the University of Salamanca and becoming a professor there, he was called upon by Juan II to become the tutor to his son, the future Enrique IV. He was also confessor to the King and was named successively to head the bishoprics of Segovia, Ávila and Cuenca. A friend of don Álvaro de Luna's, he remained constantly faithful to the King and, after the execution of Luna, was entrusted with the reins of government by Juan II during the few remaining months of that monarch's life. Under Enrique IV he held for a while the position of Royal Chancellor. His writings, besides the *Tratado de la adivinanza,* included synodal constitutions, a memorial in favor of the recently converted Jews, a treatise on sleep and dreams, another on chance and fortune, and a reworking of the *Crónica del halconero.*

In spite of the importance of his role in government and the church, Barrientos has been remembered and written about most frequently as the man who burned the library of Enrique de Villena. The charge is true, but there may have been mitigating circumstances. Villena, in his lifetime, gained a reputation for necromancy and dabbling in the black arts, and when he died in Madrid, the King ordered Fray Lope to examine his books and destroy those not compatible with Catholic beliefs (the King may also have been motivated by personal spite against his cousin). Barrientos executed the royal command and did burn some books (no one knows for certain how many), but it is also true that he kept some of them for himself and his friends. Although

Barrientos was an erudite and relatively enlightened book lover himself, the affair has marred his reputation.

The *Tratado de la adivinanza* is an attack on excessive credulity. It has little literary merit, nor is it important as a document of original thought, since most of its material is based on previous sources, especially the Church fathers. It does show the sort of superstitious practices and beliefs that existed (and still exist) and that were constantly being combatted by the Church. Lest it be thought that this was purely a theoretical work and not related to reality, it should be noted that certain enemies of don Álvaro de Luna consulted a witch to find out what fortune had in store for the royal favorite.

Concerning the different types and methods of divining.

We said that in the fifth main division we would explain the diversity of ways in which this crime is committed, that is, we would tell the types of divining or divination.

There are twenty-five main types. Hence, this part should be divided into twenty-five chapters, according to the number of types of divining, except that it is necessary to include some in the chapters of others, inasmuch as it is somewhat difficult to know how some of these depend on others.

For better knowledge, therefore, it seems advisable to draw up the following tree, whereby whoever wishes to consult it will know how all kinds of magic art derive from and depend on this term "divination," which is the genus of them all.

First, three principal divisions depend on it: the first is when evil spirits are called by express invocation; the second is done without express invocation, merely by the consideration of the arrangement of a certain thing; the third is done without express invocation and by one's own action, so that some hidden thing will become known to us.

On the first division depend five others: to wit, *prestigium,* dreams, soothsaying, necromancy and figures appearing in things that have no soul. On this fifth division depend five others: (1) geomancy, which is done on a shiny stone or polished iron or similar things; (2) hydromancy, which is done in water; (3) aeromancy, which is done in the air; (4) pyromancy, which is done in fire; (5) auspice or *auspicium,* which is done by watching birds.

On the second principal division depend two kinds: i.e., (1) astrology and (2) augury.

On the third principal division depend others that are called "with lots". From these come three others, to wit, aeromancy, scapulimancy and gyromancy; and on this third and last depend five others: the first is done with dots; the second with lead; the third with cedulas; the fourth with dice; and the fifth with a book...

> Barrientos proceeds to classify and explain the twenty-five methods of divination. The first fourteen are omitted, inasmuch as the treatment is rather monotonous and is, for the most part, repeated in the section of questions and answers concerning the licitness of various practices.

The third principal type, which is the fifteenth with respect to the lesser types, is done with the express invocation of malign spirits, only through the contemplation of certain things that come about from certain acts that men do to know some hidden future thing. This is when men cast lots of some kind, to enquire about certain future things, and this type is called divination by lots.

Divination by lots is sometimes called divisory, and this is done when lots are cast to give each person his share of something. At other times it is called consultative; this is when lots are cast to know what ought to be done. At other times it is called divinatory; this is when lots are cast to know some future, hidden thing. This last one contains three types: the first (which is the sixteenth with respect to the preceding) is called chiromancy, which means divinations done on the hand, for those who make use of this presume and attempt to know secret and coming things by lines that are on a person's hand. It is derived from a Greek word, *chiros,* which means "hand" in our language, and *mancia,* so that it means "divination done on the hand."

The second type which depends on the aforementioned, and is seventeenth with respect to the preceding, is called gyromancy, different from the above, and it is done in five ways:

The first is done by casting dots with a pen and then consulting the figures made by them.

The second is done by consulting certain figures that come from melted lead poured into water.

The third is done by certain written or unwritten *cedulas* in a secret place, considering which cedula comes to each person. This is also done with straws of unequal length, to see who gets the longer or shorter, and making decisions on this.

The fourth is done by throwing dice and looking at the spots that come up on each.

The fifth is done by taking a book which has a thread in each page, and on each page are written different kinds of fortunes; he who wants to know what is going to happen puts the book in front of himself and without deliberation pulls on one of the strings and opens the book, and makes a decision on the secret and future things he wishes to know, according to what is written on that page.

All five of these methods are called "lots"; so decides St. Thomas. Counting these five ways with the aforementioned makes twenty-five types of divination, both principal and lesser.

There are other superstitious or magic methods that are not included here, inasmuch as they come under those mentioned, such as characts and shapes and ligatures that are tied around the neck or some other limb, or, similarly, when two friends are walking together and a rock or a little child comes between them; or when someone is putting on his shoes and sneezes, he goes back to bed; or a person returns home if he stumbles when he is starting a journey. All these and similar things are superstitious ways, as is explained more extensively in the third chapter, but all can be combined and included under the above named types.

We have put these methods of divination in this treatise, in the manner previously described, not intending to lengthen the discussion of them, so as not to give cause for sinning to ignorant people who might read this book.

What has been said is sufficient for our purpose, which was to compile all the magic and superstitious ways that come under the name of divination, but since some doubts might occur to the hearers, with regard to the permission or prohibition of the preceding types, it is therefore desirable to bring up certain problems or questions here, so that doubts that may occur about this material will be briefly clarified and resolved...

Reply and solution to the first doubt and question, which is: if it is licit to divine and decide by the forecast of the stars.

To this question one should answer, according to the decision of St. Thomas, that the celestial bodies are not causes of two effects, which occur in things substantially subject to the movement of those bodies. The first thing is the effect that comes about by accident, either in human affairs or natural things. So is it proved in the book of Metaphysics, where it is shown that the thing which happens by accident has no special natural cause, as when a rock falls, the earth shakes; or when a man digs, he finds treasure. Secondly, we say that celestial bodies are not things that conform with the will, although in their arrangement they can incline men to such acts, to the extent that they impress and have influence on human bodies.

It does not follow from this, however, that there is any compulsion on free will. Therefore, if someone wishes to make a determination by the stars in these two things, that is, to know things that happen by chance and things that depend on the free will of men, he is going on a false premise, in which is mingled the operation of evil spirits, and it is therefore illicit and condemned. But to use the forecast of the stars to know future things that are caused by the movement of celestial bodies, such as rains and droughts and other things that have natural causes, it is not illicit nor a sin, as we explained at greater length in the treatise *On Chance and Fortune*.

Reply to the second question: if it is a sin to use natural things for the health of human bodies.

To this question we say that using natural things for natural, I mean corporal, sufferings, for which they have some efficacy, is not an illicit or superstitious thing, provided that signs or charects or unknown names are not mixed in or added. Such things have no efficacy to produce of themselves such effects of health. Hence, if this mixing is done, besides not being the truth, it would be an illicit and superstitious thing. So decides St. Thomas.

Reply to the third question: if signs or charects can be mixed with natural things to produce certain effects.

To this question one should reply that such a mixing should not be done, because such signs, figures and charects naturally have no efficacy at all, inasmuch as such figures are not and cannot be the cause of any natural action, and if they seem to have some effect, that comes from the illusions of evil spirits. Therefore, such signs and figures should not be used, for such use is illicit and superstitious, as St. Thomas decides.

Reply to the fourth question: if divination which is done by calling on malign spirits is licit.

To this one should reply, according to the decision of St. Thomas, that it is not licit, but rather is a grave sin for two reasons. The first is that in the invocation of evil spirits one makes an express contract with them, which is an illicit and condemned action. Against such people Isaiah wrote: *Dixistis, pepegimus fedus cum morte et cum inferno fecimus pactum,* which means: "Ye have said, 'we have made a covenant with death. And with the netherworld are we at agreement.'"

Hence, to make a covenant with evil spirits is to make a covenant with death, from which ensues the death of the soul, and consequently there follows the covenant with hell, where such people will be destined for ever and ever.

The second reason is the danger that ensues therefrom, for evil spirits always purpose in their replies the damnation and perdition of men, and, granting that they tell the truth sometimes, they do so to accustom men to believe and put faith in them until they bring them to the point of perdition.

Therefore, Athanasius, expounding on St. Luke, says that our Lord rebuked the evil spirit when He said to him *Obtumesce.* Hence the Gloss says that even though the evil spirit might speak the truth, our Lord rebuked and ordered him to be silent, so that he could not mix falsehood with truth and accustom men to listen and give him credence until they might be brought to perdition. Therefore, no one should call them nor seek their answers, for it is a grave sin to leave the advice and doctrines of Holy Scripture and seek diabolic doctrine.

If, perchance, someone wishes to argue against this, citing what is written in Holy Scripture, that Saul went to seek counsel of the soothsayer, one should reply as St. Augustine answers about this passage, as we said in the last chapter, on the third type of divination.

Answer to the fifth question: if it is licit to predict through auguries.

To this question one should reply, according to the decision of St. Thomas, that future things cannot be known by the movements and songs of birds, but that the action of brute animals is a natural instinct which comes from two causes. One is from the movement of the celestial bodies, and in this sense it is not unreasonable that the actions of animals and birds should be a sign of coming things, inasmuch as they are in conformity with the condition of the air and the celestial bodies, from which condition certain future things take place. But it is advisable to observe two points here: the first, that this consideration and these forecasts do not go beyond knowing future things that are caused by the conditions and the movements of the air and the celestial bodies; the second, that such predictions do not go beyond the things that pertain to birds and animals, which receive from the heavenly bodies a natural knowledge necessary for their preservation. Thus far can predictions be made from the movements of birds and animals and the songs of birds.

In another way, this instinct of birds and animals comes from a spiritual cause, as it seems in the dove that descended on our Lord, or the raven that fed the prophet Elijah, or the whale that swallowed Jonah. Also, such instincts come from evil spirits, who at times use the actions of birds and animals to get souls into some nonsense and false beliefs. In this sort of case, such a prediction would not be licit. And as for what is written of Joseph —that there was no one like him in the knowledge of auguries—, this should be understood, as St. Augustine concludes, with regard to the opinion that people had of him, and not that such art is permitted or approved.

Reply to the sixth question: if it is licit to look at and observe certain signs to know certain contingent future things, such as sickness or health, as doctors sometimes do.

To this question one must reply that considering the signs of future things through their determinative causes, which future things are clearly shown by such signs and causes, is not illicit, just as it is not illicit for a servant to take up the whips, when he sees that his master is angry. Similarly, to fear the harm that can come to children from those whose eyes are impaired in such a way that they might molest, and to fear such harm, is not illicit. So concludes St. Thomas in the aforementioned book and question, notwithstanding the fact that some are of the opinion that such harm to the eye cannot be caused. They hold this opinion because they do not have a perfect knowledge of natural principles, for such harm can often happen naturally. Therefore, if one knows the causes and signs of such harm, it is not illicit to observe the signs to avoid the harm.

So, too, can one know the causes of health and sickness or life and death in certain signs, and one can licitly make predictions by such causes and signs. So decides St. Thomas.

Answer to the seventh question: if it is licit to observe certain seasons, to know about what they wish to do.

In answer to this question we say that there are some things that come about through a natural progression and others that come about through will. Hence, to observe the seasons to do things that are caused by natural conditions of the elements and seasons is not a sin. Thus doctors, in caring for bodily ills, consider the movements of the celestial bodies for curative or purgative medicines, and do not sin, inasmuch as bodies and limbs are affected by the movements of the celestial bodies. But in those things that are voluntary and subject to the free will of men, it is a sin to make such observations of the seasons. For a better knowledge of the meaning of this, one should know that there are three ways of observing the seasons. One way is illicit and superstitious; this is observing the advent of things that are subject to the free will of men, such as beginning certain human deeds under a particular sign from heaven. Those who carry on such observations are reprehended by a Prophet who said: Stay and gather your soothsayers, who counted the years and the days and the months." The second observation is by way of foresight, i. e., observing the nature of the season to have an abundance of temporal fruits and avoid poverty and famine. This kind is neither praised nor reproved.

Another observation of the seasons is a pious and devout act. This is when good Christians wish to keep the feasts and praise our Lord and, especially, do works of charity as recognition of certain benefits received on such days, and therefore the Apostle says: *aliquid iudicat inter diem et diem.*

So decides Pierre de Tarentaise.

Reply to the eighth question: if it is a sin to seek into and desire to know about things that have been stolen, looking at the astrolabe or in the forecast of the stars.

To this question one should reply that inquiring into those things that properly depend on the progression of the stars and heavenly bodies, such as wishing to know if it will be hot or cold, or if it will rain or be dry, is not a sin. But to forecast about those things that are subject to the free will of men and not to the laws and progression of the stars is a grave sin, in that there ordinarily occurs the invocation of evil spirits, either expressly or tacitly, in such actions. So decides Alexander of Hales.

Reply to the ninth question: if it is licit to say certain prayers when picking herbs for sicknesses, or to put certain writings on men and animals.

To this question we say that no prayers should be said or placed, other than the Credo and the Pater Noster, and if other, superstitious things are used, it is a grave sin, as extensively determined in the *Decretum,* where one reads of a clergyman who, withdrawing to a secret place, not with the intention of invoking evil spirits, but with the desire to use the astrolabe to investigate a robbery that was committed in a church, committed a grave sin for that reason, even though his intention was good. So decides St. Thomas.

Therefore, one should not use any prayers or writings, other than those just indicated, in such acts.

One can know from experience of many people who have mixed other, illicit things in their prayers. Therefore, in such cases, one should not under the pretense of devotion exceed what is established and decided in the Laws.

Reply to the tenth question: if it is licit to hang the divine words of Holy Scripture around one's neck.

To this we say that one must consider four things in this case. First, what it is that is written and hung around the neck; for if it is to seek the help of evil spirits, this obviously seems to be illicit and superstitious. Second, one must consider if such writings have in them certain unknown or unrecognized names, under which certain illicit things could be hidden. Therefore it is not permitted, but is, rather, illicit and prohibited in the Laws, that anyone should dare to wear amulets or other writings that have any unknown words on them. Third, observe that such writing should not have any falsehood in it, for with such a document one could not ex- pect any good effect from our Lord, since He will not be a witness to falsehood. The fourth is to see to it that no vain or illicit things, such as figures or characts, are mixed with the divine words, but only the sign of the cross. So decides St. Thomas.

But you should believe that it would be more profitable to hear it in church than to wear it around your neck, for if this does not benefit you, it will benefit you less to wear it. What comes in through your ears is more efficacious than what is hanging around your neck, for that which enters through the ears and the other senses goes to the soul, but something hanging around one's neck is not an instrument that is perceived, whereby the soul can receive any wisdom.

You should also believe that having the Gospel and other divine words in one's mind is more efficacious than having letters and figures around one's neck.

However, if you observe the four conditions set forth, it is not illicit to wear such writings around your neck.

Reply to the eleventh question: if it is licit to wear the relics of Saints, or have them in any way.

To this question we say that there is the same explanation for relics of Saints as for the Gospel and holy words. Therefore, if such things are worn out of faith in the Saint to whom they pertain, it is licit; but one should beware of putting with them any other, vain thing, such as believing that it is more beneficial for the box they are kept in to be square or round or triangular. With reference to our Lord, one shape is no better than another. To believe the contrary is illicit and superstitious. So decides St. Thomas.

Reply to the twelfth question: if it is licit to charm snakes and other animals.

To this one must reply that if there is repect and consideration only for sacred words and divine virtue in such incantations, it is not illicit. But those who use such incantations have certain processes that are effective, especially in serpents, because the serpent was the first diabolic agent to deceive men. So decides St. Thomas.

Reply to the thirteenth question: if it is licit to charm children and sick people.

To this one must reply, following the decision of St. Thomas, that if no superstitious thing is done or caused to be done or said in such acts, but it is done licitly, with permissible prayers and conjurations, such, as conjuring on the cross and the Passion of our Lord and other such things, those who do it do not sin, unless they should do it after it was prohibited them by the Church, for such things are to be prohibited because superstitious things are often mixed in such acts, unless they be done by discreet and devout persons who say devout prayers over the clothing or belts, but not placing their hands on the sick, as the Gospel says. So decides St. Thomas in the aforementioned book.

Reply to the fourteenth question: if it is a sin to try to learn certain things from evil spirits.

To this question we say that it is illicit and a grave sin for two reasons: first, because even though trying to gain knowledge may in itself be good, trying to gain it in an unauthorized way, i. e., with the help of evil spirits, is not licit or good. And this is the aim of the Notorious Art, as I shall tell later in question sixteen. The second reason is that trying to know future things through evil spirits is a grave sin; first, because evil spirits do not definitely know the future, and second, because of the company that one is keeping in such a case. So decides St. Thomas.

Reply to the fifteenth question: if proof by burning iron or boiling water, which people are made to take to ascertain the truth about certain hidden crimes, is licit.

To this question we say that it is illicit and a grave sin for three reasons: first, because such a thing is done with the aim of knowing and judging hidden things, which are reserved to Divine judgment alone. The second reason is that in such cases we expect a miracle, and this is tempting God. The third reason is that it is condemned and prohibited by law. So decides St. Thomas in the aforementioned book.

Reply to the sixteenth question: if it is licit to use the observations of the Notorius Art to be able to attain knowledge.

To this question one must reply that the Notorius Art is illicit and also of no efficacy.

First, I say that the Notorious Art is illicit inasmuch as in it people use things that, as such, have no virtue to cause knowledge, such as looking at certain figures, signs and words, which the Notorious Art does not use as causes or signs ordained by God or the Church (as are the words of the Sacraments), and such are not the signs of the Notorious Art; rather, they are such as belong to the contracts that those who use this Notorious Art make with evil spirits. Therefore, this art is totally condemned and should be avoided by faithful Christians, just as the other illicit and superstitious arts that we have discussed.

In the second place, I say that this Notorious Art is vain and of no efficacy in acquiring knowledge, and this is proven thus: knowledge is gained either by a way that is natural to man or by divine inspiration, but it is never attained through the operation of evil spirits. I say that it is gained in a way that is natural to man, i. e., discovering it by himself or learning it from another. Similary, I say it is attained through divine inspiration, as is written in St. Luke: *ego dabo vobis os et sapientiae.*

Fourth, no one gains knowledge by the Notorious Art, unless it is by divine grace or gift, as the Apostle writes: *Aliis datur sermo sapientiae et scientiae, etc... haec autem omnia operatur unus atque idem spiritus, dividens singulis prout vult.*

I have said also that knowledge is never gained through the workings of evil spirits, inasmuch as it does not pertain to them to illumine our comprehension. So decides St. Thomas.

Therefore, no one should presume or endeavor to gain knowledge through such a sacrilegious and condemned art, for there are other, good ways by which one can gain much knowledge. Nor should he place faith or hope in such a vain, ineffectual thing.

Reply to the seventeenth question: if it is licit to use the designs that astrologers make.

To this question we shall say that it is not licit or permitted to use such designs, because they have no effect, unless it is through the operation of evil spirits. A sign of this is that they always have to write some other figures or characts on such designs, which cannot naturally do anything or have any effectiveness. Therefore, they are either making tacit treaties with evil spirits or they are making express invocations to them. So decides St. Thomas.

Reply to the eighteenth question: if it is licit for clergymen to strip the altars and cover the images with mourning and remove the usual lamps because of sorrow for certain violences done to the Church.

To this question one must reply that it is not licit, but is prohibited by the Law: *Ut si quicumque, etc.*

And if the person who should do so does not purge himself and do penance, he should be removed from his position, unless he did it fearing some contamination to the holy things or some subversion of the faith, and in such a case humility rather than deception is shown, as is decided in the said chapter "*quicumque*."

Similarly, it is prohibited in that chapter that any priest should dare to celebrate the mass for the dead for living people he dislikes, so that they should die sooner, nor should he make a bier in the middle of the church and hold the service for the dead, so they will soon die. If some priests do this and can be arrested, they should be removed from office. And if any layman should incite him to such a deed, both should be deposed and do penance in perpetual imprisonment. So decides the aforementioned chapter "*quicumque*."

Reply to the nineteenth question: what thing is this, that people say there are certain women called witches, who believe and say that they travel at night with Diana, goddess of the pagans, with many women riding on beasts, and travel through many towns and lands, and can be harmful or beneficial to children?

To this one must reply what Archbishop Raimundo decides on the question: that such things are the work of evil spirits who present these fantasies to the imagination of men and women. Or that the evil spirits, theologically speaking, change into different species and shapes and appear to and deceive the souls they hold captive. No one should admit such great nonsense as believing that these things happen physically, but only in dreams or through the workings of the imagination. Anyone who believes it is an infidel and worse than a pagan.

And speaking naturally, every man of sense and judgment should consider whether those witches, who say they travel through innumerable places and enter houses through cracks, leave their bodies in such acts or take them along. One cannot say that they leave them, for according to theologians and philosophers it is impossible for the soul to leave the body whenever it wants to. And if they say that they take their bodies with them, this too is impossible, because every body has three dimensions, length, width and depth, and as large as they are, so large a space do they need to enter and pass, and therefore it is impossible that they can enter through cracks and holes in houses. As for saying that they turn into geese and suck children, it is even greater nonsense to say that a man or woman can leave the form of his species and take on the form of any other. Therefore, one must believe that this is the work of the imagination and that such people have some inner capacity impaired, as we said in the treatise on dreams, in such a way that their imagination runs rampant, doing such deeds. To believe the opposite comes only from lack of judgment and from not taking into consideration the above reasons.

Therefore, women should take good care of their children, and if they die from lack of care, should not excuse themselves with witches that come in through cracks to kill them; for to affirm such stupidity would be to say that they had glorified bodies, to enter as our Lord came in to the disciples, *janus clausis*.

(Fray Lope de Barrientos, *Tratado de la adivinanza,* part V.)

MEDICINE AND HEALTH

The state of medical science in fifteenth century Spain is presented at its most appealing by the writings of Alonso Chirino, known also as Alonso García de Guadalajara. Not a great deal is known of Chirino's life; he was a doctor to Juan II and chief examiner of doctors and surgeons in the realm. One of his sons, much better known to literary history than his father, was the famous Diego de Valera, adviser to and chronicler of the Catholic Monarchs, Ferdinand and Isabel. As in the case of so many people associated with the medical profession in Spain throughout the Middle Ages and later, the Chirino family background was Jewish.

The book from which the following excerpts are taken, called by its author a *Tratado llamado menor daño de medicina (Treatise entitled the Lesser Harm of Medicine),* was first published in Seville by Jacob Cronberger in 1506, almost eighty years after the author's death. There are a number of later editions, as well as various manuscripts. Considering his official position as examiner of doctors and surgeons, Chirino's approach to his profession seems unusual. He did not place great trust in medicine, although he was evidently well versed in it, being able to cite the works of Aristotle, Hipocrates, Maimonides, Avicenna and Averroes, among others. His first book, entitled the *Espejo de medicina (Mirror of Medicine),* raised a storm of protest.

Some idea of its contents may be gained from a second work that Chirino wrote to defend himself against the attacks of his outraged colleagues. In this *Réplica (Reply)* he iterated his belief that nature is primarily responsible for the cure or death of the patient, attacked the use of astrology in medicine and listed a number of reasons why he considered medicine doubtful. He returned to these themes in the *Menor daño de Medicina,* which might best be described as a treatise on hygiene with rules for healthy living, a sort of domestic medical guide. Some of Chirino's beliefs, such as his faith in the healthful properties of vinegar and honey, still have their adherents.

On some general rules.

Every food that people have been accustomed to eat is good for those who are in good health, when they do not feel any indisposition from it and when they take it in suitable quantity, eating when the body requires it for its maintenance, according to its habit and the physical labor it perfoms. One should eat to live and not live to eat. When a person does not have an appetite, he should wait longer than usual to eat. Before eating he should get some exercise, doing all or most of the work for that day. Exercise before eating, either on foot or on horseback, is good for everyone, according to his station in life and his habits, and it should be done until warmth comes and the body and limbs feel heated. He who can wait to eat until he is truly hungry will stay out of the reach of medicine. After eating avoid all exercise and work as much as possible, and avoid converse with women as much as you can, at least for two hours. Just as exercise before eating is praised, so is it disapproved after eating, and is a cause of many illnesses.

How a man should eat a single dish and one wine at each meal.

One of the worst uses of food is to eat many different kinds at one meal, even though they may be all meat, or all fish. They are especially harmful when their qualities are contrary, as is the case with meat and fish and dairy products and so forth. It is also harmful to eat a heavy and solid food before a light and delicate one. The best thing is to eat enough of one food either boiled or roasted, at each meal. But if appetite demands that there be two dishes, eat the better and lighter one first; and if it demands that there be many dishes, see if you cannot arrange it so they are all of the same kind at each meal, such as boiled, roasted and stewed mutton. Every food that each person naturally likes very much is the most suitable for him for the most part, unless it is very harmful and contrary to all reason, as are all kinds of mushrooms and fungi, which are dangerous foods. Because of the great doubt there is concerning them, everyone should avoid them, for they are called the "delightful poison."

On using foods moderately, and thus all are good.

The person who is temperate and wise in these things will not have to pick and choose his foods, but for those who are not, and for the delicate, the inactive and those who have a weak constitution or have been sick for a long time, it is well that they eat the best foods in suitable quantity, and they should eat those that are not called good sparingly and less often, and never at supper, for they will bear them better at dinner. But it remains true that every food is good for those who are robust and just the opposite of the people mentioned above. It is, therefore, inane to defame some foods as completely bad and praise others as completely good. There are many people who avoid certain foods for this reason, saying that they cause gout and other illnesses; although many people have eaten such foods for a long time and never felt such ailments or even a part of them. And there are many people who have eaten certain foods for a long time because they have a reputation for producing certain benefits; which benefits or advantages never came to them. And in this way many other vain admonitions and threats that many doctors make are found not to be true, for it is not the condition or state of health of bodies that they are judging.

How a person should conform to his constitution in eating.

Some foods, such as kid, hens, eggs and the like, are praised in medicine, and some men find them harmful; others, such as beef, fish, game, hard-boiled eggs and the like, are not praised, and other men fare well with them. For this reason it behooves everyone to follow what pleases the nature of his own individual constitution, and what he has tried and knows is best for him and suits him most, and he should use it that way.

How eating once a day is healthy.

Those who eat any food, light or heavy, and feel some indisposition after dinner, will be well directed to omit the following supper. And if they should feel that indigestion after more dinners, they should omit more suppers. For by no means should a man who eats only once a day think that he can receive any harm or be weakened from not eating the rest of that day and night. And when food produces acidity and upset in the stomach, it is well to vomit it at once and not eat until the next day. If this happens often, it is desirable to lessen your drinking of wine as well as water and broth, and the thirstier you become, especially between meals, the sooner will you be cured. If this acidity lasts for a long time, even though you are following this regimen, try sometimes to eat three slices of bread in water before starting to eat the meal. And let no one wonder at this until he has tried it.

On foods of greater sustenance.

Foods of greater sustenance that are suitable for more robust people and are more filling and satisfying are all of the meats. Roast meat supports and maintains strength better than boiled meat, although it is harder to digest. The best of the meats are kid, veal, mutton and the whole family of hens and partridges, and whatever other meats that have a reputation of being good for delicate people. But for those who do physical labor there are beef, fresh or cured pork, venison and game, and other meats that have the reputation of engendering heavy humors. Any meat, of whatever kind. should be cut up in small pieces and chewed well, so it can more readily be digested, and this is especially desirable for delicate and inactive people. Roasted food, whether meat or fish, should not be covered right after it is taken from the fire, for this is harmful. Rather, the fumes should be allowed to escape. The same is true for boiled food, although there is greater harm with roasted. The best meats are from sheep and kids and yearling calves; the males are better than the females, young ones are better than old, and the right half is better than the left. The best of the fowls are hens and their family, and next, partridges. Beef is bad for every illness, as are all heavy, hard and wild meats. Fresh and salt pork are good for those who do a lot of physical labor and are healthy, but inactive people should not eat much of them.

Foods of lesser sustenance.

The foods of lesser sustenance and that are less filling are good fish, and the best of these are the small ones. The worst, whether large or small, are salted fish. The person who wishes to counteract the bad effects of fish, large or small, should put oil on it, and eat honey with or after it. If he wants sauces, they should be made with honey and vinegar, whether it is rocket, parsley or mustard. This mixture of honey and vinegar is good on every food it goes with, meat, fish or whatever. This, it is understood, is for healthy people. There are other foods, a small quantity of which gives much sustenance and they are not filling, such as the juices of roast meat goat's milk, and the yolks of fresh hens' eggs, although they are very bad food for anyone who has or has had the ague, and he who has had it should not eat them for two weeks after it has gone away.

On heavy and hard to digest foods, and on vegetables.

Cheese, milk and things made from it are heavy foods and not suitable for the inactive, the delicate or the sick, with the exception of goat's milk and the whey and butter from it, which are good for medicines, on the occasions that I shall discuss later. Goat's milk is good dried to cause diarrhoea, and cooked with mint to constipate. Milk is good for dessicated and tired people, and the person who eats or drinks it should not eat meat or drink wine with it. It is harmful for those who have spleen or liver ailments and for phlegmatic people, and ewe's milk is the worst. All vegetables are of slight sustenance, and he who especially eats cabbage, white-beets or spinach with the intention of loosening the bowels, should eat them slightly cooked and drink their broth; when he wants them to constipate, they should be well cooked and he should not drink the broth, and they constipate more if they are cooked in two waters. Cabbage, eggplant, lentils and olives are considered melancholic; lettuce, borage, sow-thistle and squash have the reputation of favoring the wit and warming the bile and blood. Onions increase the phlegm, and leeks are less harmful cooked with meat than raw. Garlic is good for people who work and for those who feel a lot of phlegm in the stomach, and it sharpens the appetite. Parsley and mint are good in sauces and cooked with meats, especially for those who experience some difficulty in the liver or spleen.

On the excellence of onion and oregano.

White onion, cut up and washed with water and mixed with vinegar and oregano, is good to help the digestion of food and it sharpens the appetite. Oregano with mint is good for worms, when taken while fasting. Item: oregano is good for stomach phlegm, sharpens vision and hearing, is very good for a cold head, aids the digestion and gives a good color to the face.

On Asparagus.

Asparagus clear the liver and kidneys and are good for the pain of colic in the stomach, and they cause urination. It is said that their broth kills dogs if they drink it, and people say if you sow sheep horns, asparagus will grow from them.

On Wine.

Which wines are good and how they should be used: there are so many masters and pupils of this, everywhere on earth, that it is unnecessary to deal with the subject, for no one could repeal or diminish what has been taught by them. But I do hold that every well-governed man should water his wine very much. Unwatered wine can bring more disadvantages that does well-watered wine. People who do not drink it, except at meals, are exercising healthfulness and temperance. White wines are good for promoting urination, which is a desirable purge for many people, but they are vaporous to the head for the most part and very harmful to the chest and for coughs, and for very delicate people who seem consumptive. Red wines are better for the stomach. *Aloques* (red wines mixed with white) are halfway between the reds and the whites. White wine is more suitable for a fish day than is red, but the person who suffers any kind of fluxion should avoid it at all times, because it is very vaporous for the head, and this is true especially for those who are weak-headed in any way or easily become intoxicated. It is neither temperate nor healthy to drink white and red wine at one meal; you should drink one at dinner and the other at supper or one, one day and the other, the next. Thick new wines are harmful to delicate and weak people and to those who suffer any illnesses.

On washing the feet.

One should comb his hair in the morning and evening, before supper, and once a month he should wash his feet with hot water and scrape off the calluses from the soles of his feet. This should be done before supper, or when the stomach is empty. Every morning it is good to rinse your mouth with cold water, and the same should be done after any sleep; and rinse it with wine or water after any meal, so it is clean and free of food.

How doctors know little in individual cases.

One should not censure the frequent repetition of something that is never accepted. Therefore, I still wish to repeat that all works of doctors are doubtful, and that they cure with those general rules that they find in medical lore, and in individual cases they understand little from individual knowledge. This happens especially with those fevers that are called agues. For the knowledge of whether they are simple or compound is one of the most difficult things in medical or natural consideration, where there are so many errors and doubts that they are innumerable, so much so that it is a marvel that any ague is truly and perfectly recognized by any doctor or physician, except in talking, for they can say lots of words that seem like real reasons, and thus have the blush of falsehood. For this reason, it is more usual for them to use the aforementioned general rules in these cures. Example: the medical art indeed tells how a fever should be purged if it is choleric or from the other humors, and when it is a compound of two or more humors, and what should be done when one humor is stronger than the other. I do not doubt that one should do this or that when the humor is such and such, but I do doubt very much that the doctor recognizes this in the body, except by very dubious signs, and whether he knows how to adapt the medicine to that humor or humors. And everything that was based on this doubt is doubtful and, consequently, dangerous.

On smallpox.

The fever of smallpox or measles usually happens to young people for the most part, when they feel a continuous warmth with pain in the back, and they rub their noses, and are frightened in their sleep, and feel a heaviness in the head and a redness and swelling in the eyes and a swelling of the body. These are the signs that smallpox or measles are about to break out, especially if that illness is prevalent in the area at the time. One should immediately scarify his legs and ears, if this is possible before they break out, but not after they have appeared. It is desirable to give him sweet and sour pomegranates and anything that is a mixture of sweet and sour, and not merely sweet, for even rose sugar or rose honey is better in a little watered vinegar. He should be given lentils with grape verjuice, and barley water is good. When he seems very weak, give him chicken broth and of the fruits that are in season, especially apples, cherries and melons; and bitter and sharp things are good for him, provided he does not have a cough or any dizziness. When he does, stop this and give him sugar in barley water and any other, bland fruits. One should be very careful not to cause diarrhoea, because generally bowel movements come at the end of smallpox. Therefore, do not give him an enema, unless he is very constipated, and then make it with oil and honey and with the broth of cooked barley. When the pocks start to break out the thing to watch out for most are the eyes, so they do not break out there. For this, it is desirable to drop there, with a feather, rose water in which is put a little saffron, some grains of sumach and a little of the rind of a pomegranate. Steep this in the rose water and apply it at least five times a day and night. Generally the pocks last nine days and when they begin to dry up the sickness is lessening. When they break out in the mouth or throat, and he is very hoarse, he should not be given anything sour and should eat sweet pomegranates, cleaned raisins, blanched almonds, sweet apples and every sweet and bland fruit, and he should keep cold water in his mouth and gargle with it if he can, so they will not break out in the throat and mouth, or to lessen the pain if they have appeared there. Item: when the pocks dry up, do not take them off forcibly, but anoint them with warm oil and cotton until they fall off by themselves, for if they are scratched off they will leave scars. To cure the scars, anoint frequently with the juice of white lilies mixed with sugar.

Concerning the teeth.

To clean the teeth, take ordinary salt and powdered meerschaum and brush the teeth with it, and afterwards rinse them with white wine. What cleans and whitens the teeth most, at the first time, is the *aqua fortis* that alchemists make of copperas, alum and other salts, which is used for putrid wounds and the like. For the pain of teeth and molars, the first thing is to cut down on food and wine and everything that is bad for aches of the head. To hold in the mouth, there is made a coction of camomile from Magán and coronilla in water; take a mouthful, warm. Item: a coction of oregano with wine or water, whichever is preferred. Item: a coction of hyssop in the same way. Item: to whiten and clean the teeth, make a powder of burnt egg shells, argol and burnt, ground alum; brush the teeth with them. These powders strengthen teeth that are loose, if you place them gently on the gums and teeth, being careful not to swallow them. Afterwards, rinse with wine the places that the powders touched.

(Alonso Chirino, *Tratado llamado Menor Daño de Medicina,* Part II, chapters 1 to 10; Part III, chapters 19, 5; Part IV, chapter 1; Part V, chapters 10, 13.)

LITERARY ATTITUDES

The final division of this series of translations seeks to illustrate the literary attitudes during the time of Juan II. If the political aspects of that weak king's reign present a rather sad picture of the state of the realm, this is more than compensated by an intense dedication to letters, a dedication fostered and shared by the king and his favorite as well as by the grandees who very often opposed them. Of the latter, none was more famous than Iñigo López de Mendoza, Marquis of Santillana (1398-1459), who represents more clearly than any other writer that transition between Middle Ages and Renaissance that characterized this period.

Iñigo López de Mendoza was a well-rounded leader of men, equally able to intrigue in politics, fight in battle or compose works of literature. The second son of a rich and powerful land-holding family, he inherited the leadership of his house after the deaths of his father and older brother. He took an active part in military life; he defended the frontier against the Moors of Granada and was one of the leaders in the internal struggles for power. In these he followed a devious course, sometimes opposing and sometimes supporting the King. In his youth he was allied with the Princes of Aragon against Juan II, but in 1429 and again in 1445 he fought with the latter against the invasions of the King of Navarre. For his loyalty on the occasion of the battle of Olmedo, he was granted the titles of Marquis of Santillana and Count of the Real de Manzanares. Nevertheless, his hatred for don Álvaro de Luna was bitter and constant, and he undoubtely contributed to the favorite's downfall. With the exception of this enmity, however, he seems to have been a man without serious enemies. His contemporaries wrote of him with friendship and admiration.

In literature, the Marquis of Santillana was an "amateur" in the very best sense of the word. He was not so erudite as such people as Juan de Mena or Alfonso de Cartagena, but he had a fine perception of literary values. His own creations, both in prose and verse, stamp him as the broadest and most inclusive writer of his time. His poetry ranged from the traditional, popular types of his native land to conscious imitations of the Italians, as in his allegorical works in which he adapted the externals, at least, of Dante's *Inferno*. He was the first to essay the sonnet in Castilian, although his attempts to acclimate this form were

not successful. His most appreciated poems are his *serrani-
llas,* or bucolic pieces, a genre which he elevated to the
highest level of delicate expression. Santillana collected in
his castle at Guadalajara a library of lovely and carefully
written manuscripts, the greater part of which still exist. He
was also instrumental in having a number of works translated to Spanish, for, although he probably had some knowledge of ecclesiastical Latin, he was not well enough versed
in that language to appreciate Horace or Virgil in the
original.

The first letter, below, is indicative of his desire to acquire knowledge of classical antiquity. In it, he requested
his son, Pero González de Mendoza, who was a student at
the University of Salamanca, to translate for him a Latin
version of parts of Homer's *Iliad.* The second document is
the famous *Prohemio e carta (Prologue and letter)* that Santillana sent with a collection of his verse to the Constable
don Pedro of Portugal in 1449. It is the earliest extant attempt at literary history and criticism in the Castilian
tongue.

*Don Iñigo de Mendoza, Marquis of Santillana and Count
of the Real, sends greetings to don Pero González de
Mendoza, protonotary, his son.*

I have received just the other day, through a relative and friend
of mine who has recently come from Italy, certain books and
writings which I believe are the first, second, third or fourth,
and part of the tenth book of that prince of poets, Homer, and of the
Trojan history which he composed and named the *Iliad,* translated
out of the Greek to Latin by Leonardo de Arezzo and Pietro Candido, of Milan. And although we have quite a full and extensive
account of these matters through Guido delle Colonne and the accounts of the Greek Dictys and the Phrygian Dares, it will be an
agreeable thing for me to see the work of such an eminent man
and almost sovereign prince of poets, especially concerning a military encounter or war which is thought to have been the greatest
and most ancient in the world. Therefore, although you have enough
work to do with your studies, as a consolation to me and for the
profit of myself and others, I heartily beg you to put your hand to
it; and since the main and, I believe, the most difficult port has

been passed by those two excellent men, do you pass the second, which is to bring it from the Latin language to our Castilian tongue.

Now I know well enough, as has happened to me before with you and others, that you will say that the greater part, or almost all, of the sweetness and loveliness is retained in the Latin words and expressions; in reply to which, although I do not know Latin, because I did not learn it, I do truly believe that the books of Holy Scripture, the Old and New Testaments, were written in Hebrew before they were in Latin, and in Latin before the other languages in which they are today read by everyone and give doctrine and instruction to all peoples; and the same is true of many histories, fabulous narratives and poems. For it would be most unlikely now that, after so many years and no few hardships, I should try to struggle with the Latin tongue, even though Tully affirms that Cato (I think it was he of Utica) learned Greek at the age of eighty; but Cato was alone and outstanding among the human race in this and many other things.

Since we cannot have what we want, let us want what we can have. And if we lack the forms, let us be content with the substance. It has been at my request and urging, before anyone else's, that certain poems have been translated to the vernacular in these realms, such as Virgil's *Aeneid,* the main book of Ovid's *Transformations,* the *Tragedies* of Lucius Annaeus Seneca and many other things in which I have taken and still take delight, and they offer a singular respite to the vexations and travails that the world continually brings, especially in these realms in which we live. Therefore, if you will accept this task, do not doubt that this work will be more pleasing to me than all the others, first because of the excellence of the subject matter and the clarity of the poet, and then because of the translator. May every day be good to you.

From my city of Buytrago, etc.

Here begins the Prologue and letter that the Marquis of Santillana sent to the Constable of Portugal with his works.

To the illustrious lord don Pedro, most magnificent Constable of Portugal, the Marquis of Santillana, Count of the Real, etc. sends greetings, peace and due praise.

These past days, Alvar González de Alcántara, an attendant and retainer in the household of my lord Prince Pedro, illustrious Duke of Coimbra, your father, requested me on your behalf, sire, to send your Excellency my poetic compositions and songs. In truth, sire, I would be willing to accomodate your noble Grace in other deeds of greater importance, even though they were more laborious to me; for these works, or at least most of them, are not on such subjects nor so well formed and crafted as to seem worthy of memorable record. Because, sire, as the Apostle says: *Cum essem paruulus, cogitabam ut paruulus, loquebar ut paruulus.* For these lighthearted and jocose things go well with the season of youth, that is, with fancy dress, jousting, dancing and other such courtly exercises. And so, sire, many things are now pleasing to you which no longer please, nor should please, me. But, most virtuous lord, protesting that my will is and will be only what I have said, and so that your will may prevail without hindrance and your command be done, I have caused to be sought out here and there, in books and collections of others, and to be written down in order, as I composed them, these works that I am sending you in this small volume.

But even though these little works of mine that you request, sire, are so inadequate, and perchance even more so than I consider them, I do wish to inform you that I am very pleased that you like all things that come under this canon of poetic song; I am assured of this both by your gracious requests and by certain exquisite things that I have seen composed by your prudence; since it is certain that this is a celestial zeal, a divine affection, an insatiable food for the spirit, and just as matter seeks form and anything imperfect seeks perfection, so has this science of poetry and Gay Science never been sought out nor found except by exquisite souls, lucid talents and elevated spirits.

And what is poetry, which we in our common tongue call the Gay Science, except a fiction of useful things, covered or veiled with a very beautiful wrapping, composed, separated and scanned by a certain count, quantity and measure? And certainly, most virtuous lord, those who would think or say that such things consist in and tend only to vanity and lewdness are in error: for just as fertile gardens abound and give suitable fruits for all seasons of the year, so do well born and learned men, in whom these sciences are infused from on high, use the exercise thereof according to the season. And if by chance sciences are desirable, as Tully holds, which of all is the most excellent, noble and worthy of men? Or which is most available to all levels of humanity? For who clarifies, points out and makes manifest their obscurities and secrets, but sweet eloquence and handsome speech, whether in verse or prose?

The excellence of poems and verse over ordinary prose is obvious, except only to those who seek to acquire haughty honors with unjust obstinacy. And so, following the path of the stoics, who very diligently inquired into the origin and causes of things, I am encouraged to say that poetry has precedence over prose in time, perfection and authority. Isidore of Cartagena, holy bishop of Seville, so proves and attests, and holds that the first person who composed poetry was Moses, for he sang and prophesied the coming of the Messiah in verse; and after him, Joshua sang in praise of the conquest of Gibeon. David celebrated in verse the victory over the Philistines and the restitution of the Ark of the Covenant, and all five books of the Psalter. For this reason, the Hebrews even dare affirm that we cannot enjoy so well as they the full measure of their sweetness. Solomon composed his proverbs in verse and certain things in Job are written in poetry, especially the words of comfort that his friends answered him in his vexations.

Among the Greeks, they say that the first were Hecataeus of Miletus, and after him, Pherecydes of Syros and Homer, although Dante calls the latter the supreme poet. Of the Latins, Ennius was the first, although Virgil is considered to hold the supremacy in the Latin tongue, and so does it please Dante, where he says, in the name of the Mantuan Sordello: *O gloria de' latin, per cui mostrò ciò que potea la lingua nostra, o pregio eterno del loco ond' io fui.*

And so I conclude that this poetic science is agreeable first to God, and them to the whole lineage and race of man. Cassiodorus affirms it in the book of *Varias Causas,* when he says: every splendor of eloquence and every manner or means of poetry or poetic locution, every variety of honest speech had their beginning in divine writings. This is sung in divine temples, and is received with joy and pleasure in imperial courts and royal palaces. The city squares, the shops, festivals, opulent feasts are as if mute and silent without it.

What are those things in which, I dare say, this art does not mediate and serve as necessary? Epithalamia, which are songs that are sung in praise of the bride and groom at weddings, are composed in verse, and in one degree or another still serve shepherds in a certain way, and are those poems which the poets call bucolics. In other times, elegiac verses were sung at the funerals and burials of the dead, and they still persist in some places, under the name of dirges. In this form did Jeremiah lament the destruction of Jerusalem. The emperors Gaius Caesar, Octavianus Augustus, Tiberius and Titus wrote marvelous verses and enjoyed every manner of poetry.

But let us leave ancient histories now, to draw closer to our own times. King Robert of Naples, a fair and virtuous Prince, was so pleased with this science that he kept with him for a considerable time at Castil Nuovo in Naples that laureate poet, Francesco Petrarca, who flourished in the same epoch, with whom he conferred and chatted often concerning these arts, so that he was considered very much a favorite of his; and he is said to have composed there many of his works, both in Latin and in the vernacular, and among others, the book of *Rerum memorandarum* and his eclogues and many sonnets, especially the one he wrote at the death of this same king, which begins: *Rotta è l'alta colonna e 'l verde Lauro,* etc. Giovanni Boccaccio, an excellent poet and renowned prose writer, affirms that King John of Cyprus was more given to the study of this graceful science than to any others, and so he seems to show in the preface to his book on the genealogy of the pagan gods, speaking with the Lord of Parma, messenger or ambassador of the King.

How then, or in what manner, most virtuous Lord, these sciences first came to the hand of writers in the Romance or vernacular languages would, I think, be a difficult inquiry and troublesome investigation. But leaving aside now the regions, lands and territories most distant and separated from us, it is not to be doubted that these sciences have been acclimated and have always been in use in all areas, and in many of them in these three degrees, to wit, sublime, mediocre and lowest. Sublime might be applied to those who wrote their works in Greek or Latin, I mean in verse of course. A mediocre level was used by those who wrote in the vernacular, such as Guido Guinicelli of Bologna or the Provençal Arnaut Daniel. Although I have not seen any work by these men, some say that they were the first to write terza rima and even sonnets in Romance. And as the philosopher says, of first things, first is speculation. Lowest are those who without any order, rule or measure compose those ballads and songs in which people of low degree and servile condition take pleasure. After Guido and Arnaut Daniel, Dante elegantly wrote in terza rima his three comedies, the *Inferno, Purgatory* and *Paradise*; Francesco Petrarca his *Triumphs*; Cecco d'Ascoli the book *De proprietatibus rerum*; and Giovanni Boccaccio the book entitled the *Nimphale,* although he joined to it prose passages of great eloquence in the manner of the consolatory Boethius. These and many others wrote in the Italian language other types of verse that are called sonnets and moral songs.

These arts, I believe, spread from the lands of the Languedocians to the Gauls and to this furthermost and western region which is our Spain, where they have been practiced quite prudently and handsomely. The Gauls and French wrote rimes and poetry in diverse manners, which differ in the number of feet or lines; but the quantity or number of syllables in terza rima and sonnets and moral songs are equal to the ballads, although in some (of one type or another) there are certain truncated feet which we call half feet and the Provençals, French and also the Catalans term *bioques.*

Among the French there have been men very learned and famous in these arts; for Master Guillaume de Lorris wrote the *Roman de la Rose,* wherein, it is said, the art of love is all enclosed, and Master Jean Clopinel, a native of the city of Meun, completed it. Machaut, also, wrote a great book of ballads, songs, rondels, lays, virelays, and set many of them to music. Otho de Grandson, a vigorous and very virtuous knight, wrote well and sweetly in this art. Master Alain Chartier, a very illustrious modern poet and secretary to this King Louis of France, composed and sang in verse with great eloquence, and wrote the *Livre des quatre dames,* the *Belle dame sans merci,* the *Reveil-matin,* the *Grand pastora,* the *Breviaire des nobles* and the *Hospital d'amour,* things that are, to be sure, very beautiful and pleasant to hear.

I prefer the Italians to the French, subject to correction by someone who knows more, only in that their works show them to be of higher genius, and they adorn and compose them with lovely and unusual stories; and I prefer the French over the Italians in observing the rules of the art, concerning which the Italians make no mention, except for measure and rime. They also write music for their works and sing them in sweet and diverse ways, and they are so familiar with music and are so practiced in it, that it seems that among them must have been born those great philosophers Orpheus, Pithagoras and Empedocles, who, as some describe, placated not only human wrath but even the furies of hell with the sonorous melodies and sweet modulations of their songs. And who doubts that just as green leaves in the spring time decorate and adorn the bare trees, so do sweet voices and lovely sounds adorn and accompany every rime, meter and verse, of whatever style, quantity and measure?

The Catalans, Valencians and also some Aragonese have been and are great exponents of this art. They wrote first in rimed ballads, which are many-syllabled refrains, with some riming and others not. After this, they used the composition of ten syllable couplets, in the manner of the Provençals. There have been among them some famous men, both in the conceits and in versification. Guillem de Bergadá, a generous and noble knight, and Pau de Bellviure gained great fame among them. Mosén Pero March, the old, a valiant and honorable knight, composed very excellent works, and among other things, wrote proverbs of great moral worth. In our own times flourished Mosén Jordi de San Jordi, a prudent knight who, to be sure, composed very beautiful things which he himself set to music, for he was an excellent musician. He composed, among others, a *canción de opósitos* which begins: *Tots jorns aprenc e desaprenc ensems.* He wrote the *Passió d'amor,* in which he collected many good, old songs, of those poets whom I have just named and others. Mosén Febrer wrote noble works, and some say he translated Dante from the Florentine tongue to Catalan, without changing a whit the order of the meter and rime. Mosén Ausías March, who is still alive, is a great troubador and a man of very elevated spirit.

Among ourselves, verse was first used in various forms, as in the *Libro de Alexandre,* the *Votos del pavón* and also the *Libro del Arcipreste de Hita*; Pero López de Ayala, the old, wrote a book in this style, which he composed on the manners of the palace, which is called the *Rimos.* Then they discovered this style which is called *arte mayor* and the *arte común,* I believe, in the realms of Galicia and Portugal, where undoubtedly the exercise of these sciences was acclimated more than in any other regions and provinces

of Spain, to such an extent that, not long ago, any poets and troubadors of these parts, whether Castilians, Andalusians or from Extremadura, composed all their works in the Galician or Portuguese
tongue, and it is true that from them we get the terms of the art, such
as *maestría mayor* and *menor, encadenados, lexapren* and *mansobre.*

I remember, most magnificent lord, that when I was at a not
very advanced age, but quite a young boy, in the care of my grand-
mother, doña Mencía de Cisneros, I saw among other books a large
volume of Portuguese and Galician songs, bucolics and compositions,
the greater part of which were by King Dinis of Portugal (I believe,
sire, he was your great-grandfather), whose works have been praised, by those who have read them, for subtle conceits and graceful
and sweet words. There were others by Joan Soarez de Pavía, who
is said to have died in Galicia for love of a princess of Portugal,
and by Fernán González of Sanabria. After them came Vasco Peres
de Camões, Fernán Casquicio and that great lover, Macías, of whom
only four poems are to be found, although they are certainly amorous and of very beautiful expressions: these are: *Cativo de minha
tristura, Amor cruel e brioso, Señora, en quien fiança* and *Prouey
de buscar mesura.*

In this kingdom of Castile, King Alfonso the Sage was skilled in
poetry; I have met people who have seen compositions of his, and
it is also said that he wrote distinguished poetry in Latin. After these
people came don Juan de la Cerda, and my grandfather, Pero González de Mendoza. The latter wrote good poems, among them *Pero
te sirvo sin arte* and another to the nuns of la Zaydia, at the time
that King Pedro was besieging Valencia; it begins: *A las riberas
de un río.* He employed a method of composing poems, something
like Plautine and Terentian scenes, both in rondolets and in bucolic
poems.

There also lived at this time a Jew named Rabbi Sem Tob;
he wrote very good things, and among them his *Proverbios morales,*
which truly have very commendable maxims. I have included him
in the number of such noble people as a great troubador, for as he
says in one of his proverbs:

> The goshawk is no less valued
> for being born in a base nest,

> nor are good proverbs less worthy
> because it's a Jew who says them.

Alfonso González de Castro, a native of this city of Guadalajara, composed very well and wrote these poems: *Con tan alto poderío* and *Vedes que descortesía*. Next, in the time of King Juan, lived the Archdean of Toro, who wrote *Crueldad e trocamento* and another poem that says: *De quien cuydo e cuydé*. And Garci Ferrandes de Gerena.

Since the time of King Enrique, of glorious memory, father of our lord, the King, and continuing until our own times, this science has been elevated to new heights of elegance, and there have been very learned men in this art, especially Alfonso Alvarez de Illescas, a great troubador, to whom one might apply what a great historian wrote in praise of Ovid, i. e., that all his sayings and words were verse. He wrote so many songs and poems that our proceedings would indeed be long and diffuse if we were to relate extensively merely the main ones. For this reason, and because his works are so well known everywhere, we shall go on to Francisco Imperial, whom I would not call a versifier or troubador, but a poet, for it is certain that if anyone in these western regions merited the reward of that triumphant laurel wreath, praising all others, it was he. At the birth of the King, our lord, he wrote that famous poem *En dos setecientos,* and many other pleasing and praiseworthy things.

Fernán Sánchez Calavera, Knight Commander of the Order of Calatrava, composed very good poems. Don Pero Vélez de Guevara, my uncle, a pleasing and noble knight, also wrote graceful poems and songs.

My uncle, Fernán Pérez de Guzmán, a knight learned in every good doctrine, has composed many things in verse, among them, that epitaph for the grave of my lord the Admiral, don Diego Hurtado, which begins: *Hombre que vienes aquí de presente.* He made many other poems and love songs, and just a little while ago wrote proverbs of great advice, and another very useful and well written work, *De las quatro virtudes cardinales.*

The most excellent Duke Fadrique, my lord and brother [-*in-law*], was very fond of this science and wrote quite graceful songs and poems, and kept in his household great troubadors, especially

Fernán Rodríguez Portocarrero, Juan de Gayoso and Alfonso de Moraña. Ferrán Manuel de Lando, an honorable knight, wrote many fine poetic things; he, more than anyone else, emulated Francisco Imperial; he wrote fine songs in praise of our Lady; he also composed some well ordered invectives against Alfonso Alvarez, on diverse subjects.

I shall not name those who have written or are writing in our own times, because I am sure that you, most noble lord, know about all of them; and do not be surprised, sire, that I have chronicled so extensively both the ancients and our own writers and some of their poems and songs, so that it might seem to have arisen from idleness. My age, no less than the disturbed times, gives the lie to this. Rather is it that, as they pleased me in youth, so did I discover them now, when they seemed necessary. For as the poet Ovid writes: *Quem nova concepit olla seruabit odorem.*

But of all these people, most excellent lord, —Italians as well as Provençals, Languedocians, Catalans, Castilians, Portuguese, and Galicians and other nations— the Cisalpine Gauls and the inhabitants of the province of Aquitaine excelled and stood out in extolling and honoring these arts. I refrain now from relating how, inasmuch as this has already been mentioned in the prologue to my Proverbs. From these and many other things that could be amplified and explained by me, and even more so by someone more knowledgeable, your Excellency will be able to perceive and recognize in what repute, esteem and praise these sciences should be held and how much you, most virtuous lord, should esteem that you have been received, not undeservedly, at such a youthful age in the company of those maidens who incessantly dance around the fountain of Helicon. Therefore, sire, I urge and advise your Excellency as earnestly as I can that, both in the search for beautiful poems and in their polished order and rule, your very lofty perception and pen should not cease as long as Clotho spins the yarn, so that when Antropos cuts off the fabric, you will obtain Delphic no less than martial honors and glories.

(Iñigo López de Mendoza, *El Marqués de Santillana a su hijo* and *Prohemio e carta.*)

APPENDIX I

ENGLISH TRANSLATION OF WORKS USED

DÍEZ DE GAMES, GUTIERRE, *The Unconquered Knight,* translated and selected from *El Victorial,* by Joan Evans (Broadway Medieval Library, London, 1928.)

MARTÍNEZ DE TOLEDO, Alfonso, *Little Sermons on Sin, The Archpriest of Talavera,* Translated by Lesley Byrd Simpson (University of California Press, Berkeley and Los Angeles, 1959.)

Martínez de Toledo, Alonso, *Arcipreste de Talavera, Corvacho, o Reprobación del Amor Mundano,* edición, prólogo y notas por Martín de Riquer (Barcelona, 1949).

Pérez de Guzmán, Fernán, *Generaciones y Semblanzas* (Colección Austral, Buenos Aires - México, 1947).

Rodríguez Delena, Pedro, *Libro del Passo Honroso,* facsimile of the edition of Salamanca, 1588, by A. M. Huntington (New York, 1902).

Tafur, Pero, *Andanças e Viajes por diversas partes del mundo avidos,* ed. por M. Jiménez de la Espada (Colección de Libros españoles raros o curiosos, tomo 8, 1 y 2, Madrid, 1874).

Villena, Enrique de, *Arte Cisoria, Arte de trinchar o cortar con cuchillo carnes y demás viandas,* prefacio y apéndice-glosario por Enrique Díaz-Retg (Barcelona, 1948).

Villena, Enrique de, *Los doze Trabajos de Hércules,* prólogo y notas de Margherita Morreale (Madrid, 1958).